Firefly Lanterns

Firefly Lanterns

Twelve Years in Kyōto

Published by Shanti Arts Publishing

Shanti Arts LLC | 193 Hillside Road
Brunswick, Maine 04011 | shantiarts.com

Cover image: Firefly Lanterns by John Einarsen,
and used with his permission

Printed in the United States of America

ISBN: 978-1-951651-98-5 (softcover)

Library of Congress Control Number: 2021944300

Firefly Lante

Twelve Years in F

Margaret Chu

Margaret Chu

SHANTI ARTS PUBL

BRUNSWICK, M

For John . . .

*Forty-nine years together
and we're still
having adventures*

Contents

The Pond Is Still There, But Smaller

Introduction

In 1977, my husband and I embarked on what turned out to be a two-year odyssey, traveling overland through Asia. We rode on buses, bemos, rickshaws, and horses—taking in the sights, sounds, and smells around us. Each country challenged us to learn a new language, culture, and monetary system. We traveled slowly, spending many weeks in each country, and months in Greece, Afghanistan, India, Nepal, Borneo, and Bali.

When we returned to the U.S. in 1979, we agreed that we wanted to live and work in a different culture for an extended period. We chose Japan. John had been practicing *aikido* and was fascinated by Japanese arts. I was drawn to the subtleties of Japanese poetry and to a culture that celebrated the beauty of everyday life. So, in 1980, unencumbered by children or jobs, we once again said good-bye to our friends and family and set off to the Land of Wa.

Arriving in Kyōto during rainy season, we quickly found teaching jobs and a place to housesit for the summer. Once settled into our permanent home in Ichō-da-chō, we immersed ourselves in the joys and challenges of living in a traditional Japanese house. I studied the arts of *ikebana* (flower arrangement) and *hanga* (woodblock printing). We both found teaching positions at universities, and when it was time to renew our contracts, we would agree to stay another year.

When we retuned to the U.S. in 1992, friends pressed us for stories about our "exotic" lives in Kyōto. Rereading journals and letters home, I began to write my recollections in the Japanese form called *haibun*, a combination of prose and haiku. *Haibun* was made famous by Japanese haiku master Matsuo Bashō in his 1694 travel journal *Oku no Hosomichi (The Narrow Road to the Deep North)*, in which he describes the places and people he encountered on his perilous journey.

Firefly Lanterns is an inner journey. Told from the viewpoint of an American woman in the twentieth century, it offers a glimpse into the life of a *gaijin* (literally: "outside person") with humorous ("*Gaijin* Gardening"), embarrassing ("At the *Sentō*"), and heartbreaking ("Sensei") stories. Enriched by my growing knowedge of Japanese history and culture, I imagine scenes, such as Sen no Rikyū's last tea ceremony and the life of Ono no Komachi, a poetess from the ninth century. In a more contemporary vein, I also recount interactions with my colleagues, students, and Japanese friends.

No book steeped in Japanese tradition would be complete without meditations on the seasons. The book begins with our arrival during rainy season ("Plum Rain"). On a hot summer evening, I'm enchanted by raccoon dogs frolicking in our garden ("Bewitched by *Tanuki*"). In autumn, I visit a mountain temple with its famous ceiling stained with samurai blood ("Faint Profiles") and in winter, hike alone in snowfields ("In the Japan Alps"). From our house at the edge of ricefields, we observe the planting and later enjoy the harvest as Lady Bountiful wheels her cart through the neighborhood selling her vegetables.

The title, *Firefly Lanterns*, refers not to actual lanterns, but to bell-shaped flowers growing in the Japanese countryside. Their name, *hotaru bukuro*, translates as "firefly pouches." In early summer, families capture fireflies with nets and insert them into the flowers' petals, creating miniature lanterns. This custom has been one of the pleasures of farming families from ancient times.

Firefly Lanterns is divided into two sections: Kyōto Days 1980-1992 and The Pond is Still There, But Smaller—*haibun* written during several return visits. You'll find a glossary of seventy Japanese words at the end to provide cultural context and more fully welcome you into our wonderful journey.

SUNLIGHT ON TATAMI

Kyōto 1980–1992

Plum Rain *(Tsuyu)*

*J*ohn and I arrive in Kyōto in mid-June, the beginning of *tsuyu*. The literal translation, "plum rain," brings to mind green plums viewed through a canopy of verdant leaves. Very romantic for this unwelcome nonseason between spring and summer. Even the Japanese, who accept most things with equanimity, begin to complain. Housewives fan themselves in a frenzy, intoning *"mushi atsui, mushi atsui"* like a Buddhist sutra that would, if repeated often enough, bring relief from suffering. *"Mushi atsui,"* steamy hot. This onomatopoeic phrase reminds John and me of soggy New England summers. But this is worse.

During *tsuyu* everything sweats, even lifeless things like the bamboo railings in our traditional Japanese house. Leather shoes grow furry with mold, especially when left in a dark corner of the entryway. *Futon* absorb moisture until they compact into hard, damp pallets. Usually, they can be aired outside, but not during *tsuyu* with its constant drizzle. We have no clothes dryer. During breaks in the rain, we thread our laundry onto a bamboo pole, and then hang the pole on wooden supports outside the second-story window.

Insects thrive in the damp heat. Mosquitoes hatch, along with polliwogs, in the newly-flooded rice fields behind our house. Then, right on schedule, school children with red or yellow caps parade like rows of brilliant tulips along the path. Out come the nets and jars. Plop they go, one by one, into the flooded fields to gather polliwogs and bring them back to the classroom.

Watching from our kitchen window, I am reminded of Bashō's famous haiku: "old pond / a frog jumps in / sound of water," and write:

> rice paddy
> polliwogs snatched in nets
> squeals of children

I sit at my writing desk trying to stay cool in my cotton *yukata* robe. The pink-petaled peony releases its perfume into the still air.

> all at once
> peony petals drop
> clap of thunder

Mosquitoes, spiders, ants. We are plagued by insects that find their way into the leaks and crevices of our old Japanese house.

> they have discovered
> my flowered kimono
> those relentless ants

Even worse is the dreaded *mukade*. The centipede's sting can kill a baby. During *tsuyu*, *mukade* migrate to dry, dark places. One day, while reaching into the back of the closet for something, I felt a prick. When I pulled my hand back, I saw a six-inch long centipede curled around my finger.

Cicadas choose this season to emerge. After nine years underground, they discard their exoskeletons, ghostly skins left clinging to the branches. Their song, a continuous buzz that resounds in the dull heat.

    sawing afternoon
    into evening
    cicadas

Meditation on *Sarasōju*

When the Buddha died, there were two *sarasōju* (sal) trees growing at each of the cardinal points surrounding his bier. A cutting from one of these was brought to Kyōto and planted in a small garden at Torin-in Temple where it blooms every year in early July.

A light rain is falling, cooling off the sultry heat of early summer in Kyōto. As I walk up the stone pathway to Torin-in, I can just make out the fragile blossoms of the *sarasōju* tree on the other side of the wall. Before going inside the temple, I remove my shoes and leave my umbrella in the stand in the entryway next to the others.

folding up
my paper umbrella
closed petals

I walk across the *tatami* mat room and sit in a far corner, away
from the flock of Japanese women who are exclaiming *"Kirei, ne!"*
Beautiful! We have all come here to enjoy the transient beauty of
sarasōju, some of us more vocally than others.

sarasōju blossoms
in the morning
shining with dew
in the evening
moldering

The sound of rain is refreshing, but it is weighing down the
delicate flowers.

moment by moment
rain loosens their hold
on the mother tree

They fall softly on the moss, one by one. I watch them, lost in reverie.
Suddenly I am startled by a deep croaking sound, and then another.
At the same time, my eyes fill with the beauty of hydrangeas.

beyond the temple wall
a bullfrog croaks
blue, blue *ajisai*

noisy bulbulls
suck nectar from flowers
that live only one day

Flapping their wings and fighting for the exotic nectar

      irreverent birds
      knock down the flowers
      before their time

      trying to guess
      which flower
      will drop off next

The falling blossoms shift my attention downward to the display on the moss. Their arrangement looks suspiciously like the photograph on the pamphlet taken last year. I imagine the head priest or gardener rearranging the blossoms every morning before the temple opens.

> spaced so evenly
> did they really fall randomly
> from the branches

In the grayness of the afternoon, the white of the *sarasōju* is so bright and the moss luxuriantly green. My eyes stray to the wall with its restful patina of age; it reminds me of my favorite wall at Ryōan-ji.

> rain-soaked moss
> on the temple wall
> a blush of rust

From the wall composed of many rocks, I focus on a single rock in the garden, which is unusual because of its elegant boat-like shape.

> *sarasōju* fall
> hollows in the rock
> fill with rain

Each blossom has fallen at a different time today. Those fallen early this morning are already brown, others are browning at the edges, and the most recent ones still look fresh.

> in different stages
> of decay, yet
> each one perfect

The temple priest rings the bell to indicate that it's closing time. Looking around, I'm surprised to discover that I am the only one there, completely absorbed in this garden of impermanence.

closing time
but waiting for my blossom
to
fall

Yu-mo-a

*T*onight we are the guests of Ishihara Sensei, who is hosting a Japanese-style banquet for the American haiku poet delegates. Ushered into a private room, we attempt to fold our long legs under the low tables as gracefully as possible. The day has been full and satisfying, with an expedition to Tōshōgu Shrine and the Tōkyō University Botanical Garden, where we viewed the last cherry blossoms of the year.

After we finish a delicious meal, Ishihara Sensei stands up to tell us about his philosophy of *naikan zokei*, introspective shaping or looking inward at the landscape of the human mind. He

emphasizes the importance of expressing truth through humor. Rather than using an original Japanese word, he says *"yu-mo-a,"* which is adapted from the English.

I stretch out my legs and close my eyes to better absorb his words. Not his words, but rather the intuitive meanings behind them. For he is like a Zen master offering insights to a roomful of receptive disciples. "The first line of a poem comes from heaven." "The *kigo* is a window to the mind." Though intriguing, I allow these ideas to slide across my mind, careful not to let them catch on any spokes. Just let the wheel turn round and around and trust that it is moving toward understanding. "To tell the truth as if it were false. True humor does not have the artificial manipulation of fiction." I look up at the ceiling of the banquet room, decorated with mirrors and plastic cherry blossoms. And, in the spirit of Ishihara Sensei's *yu-mo-a*, I write

> artificial blossoms
> dangle from the ceiling
>   forever

Bewitched by *Tanuki*

I sit on the tatami with the *shōji* wide open in hopes of catching a cool breeze. Suddenly, I'm startled by a movement from the garden. There, just six feet away, a furry animal stares back at me. We hold each other's gaze until, utterly fearless, it finally turns away.

Can this be a *tanuki*, the raccoon dog that Lafcadio Hearn writes about in his *Tales of the Mysterious?* Japanese translate *tanuki* as badger, but they look more like raccoons with their black masks and brown fur, except they are smaller, leaner, and have longer legs. In Japanese folklore, the *tanuki* is a trickster. One of its favorite pranks is to transform itself into another animal—or even a human.

A few days later, I see it again. Though I've been thinking of it as a male, it is definitely female, a nursing mother with pink extended nipples. She comes closer this time; I move slowly toward her, ready to close the *shōji* if she tries to enter the house. All I can think of are those sharp teeth that chewed up the leather sandals I left outside one night. But Mama holds her ground, then turns and lumbers away. I throw out some fish scraps and am happy to see them gone in the morning. At dusk I hear a rustle in the garden and turn just in time to see a baby *tanuki* skitter across the moss. Then two others, like puppies, frolicking. One grabs my gardening glove and tears around with it, playing keep-away. I laugh out loud at their antics. Then they begin to scratch up the moss. They are adorable, but I have mixed feelings about them destroying our moss garden.

I am so excited that I call my friend, Michiko. "I have *tanuki* in my garden!"

"Impossible," she says. "Maybe you can find a *tanuki* in the countryside, but never in the city."

The next morning I am jolted awake by a squawk. Dressing quickly, I follow the sound to the abandoned house across the street. A baby *tanuki* has fallen into a deep hole. Mama and her two pups watch from a distance as I try to help. But the hole is too deep and narrow to go down and rescue him. I prop up a wooden plank into the hole hoping that, with those sharp claws, he'll be able to climb out.

     from a deep hole
     baby *tanuki* screeching
     ravens circle

At dusk, the *tanuki* come once again to play in the garden and to eat the rice I've left out for them. I feel sad seeing only two babies instead of three. Mama crouches nearby and seems unconcerned. Do animals mourn the death of their offspring?

The following evening is the annual fire festival at Tanuki-dani in the East Hills of Kyōto. To get to the Raccoon Dog Temple, you must walk through a cedar forest, then climb two hundred and fifty stone steps to the top of the mountain. Although it's drizzling, I feel I should go there to say a prayer for the baby *tanuki* who died.

They are impressive, these old folks making their way up to receive the priest's blessing. Some have canes, others pull themselves up, step by step, grasping the railing. Our ascent is punctuated by the beat of ancient drums played by *yamabushi*, wandering Shinto priests. Some of them carry huge conch shells, which they blow through to ward off evil. The sound is eerie, like a grieving animal.

At the top of the mountain, a crowd gathers around a bonfire in the center of the courtyard. The *yamabushi* are dressed in robes with *tanuki* pelts fastened to a silk cord round their waists and hanging in the back, like a tail. Forming a circle, they chant sutras, joined by attendees who recite religious texts from memory. Once the fire's burned down, priests from Tanuki-dani spread the embers with heavy wooden rakes. *Yamabushi* and Buddhists pilgrims, identified by their white robes, walk across first. Barefoot. I take my place at the end of the long line, hoping that by the time my turn comes the coals will have been well tramped. When I finally walk across the coals, I am surprised that I feel no pain. To the contrary. Reaching the other side, I feel cleansed and renewed.

I take my time descending the stone steps back down the mountain. The sky has cleared and a full moon appears through gaps in the trees. Dim light from paper lanterns guides my way. I feel as though I'm under the *tanuki's* spell.

The following evening, as usual, I throw chicken scraps out into the garden. And once again, the *tanuki* come—Mama and her pups. *Four* pups. Where did the fourth one come from? Not only did the third baby not die, but it seems to have reproduced itself.

> in my sandals
> the blessed ashes
> of Raccoon Dog Temple

Lovers, Molesters, and Maidens

teacher's question
hangs in the drowsy classroom
a crow answers

The heat and humidity are stifling, and we still have two weeks of classes before summer vacation. At least here at Kyōto Seika College, I can open the windows and get some mountain air. These young women are exhausting with their need to be entertained. Today, feeling nostalgic, I begin rambling about my experiences hitchhiking from Spain to England when I was twenty. How I borrowed a Frenchman's surfboard in Guethary, got wiped out by the waves, and nearly drowned. Doctors stitched up my forehead, which I'd hit on the fin of the surfboard. My students, who think all Americans are wealthy, are shocked to hear that my friend had to take out the stitches because I couldn't afford to pay a doctor. They all listen today—even ask questions—and I have a good time reminiscing.

In the next Beginner English class, I go back to the textbook and set up a role-playing exercise for the students: making a telephone date, then meeting at a restaurant. After I explain the vocabulary and structure of the skit, they ask me for some American men's names, besides Michael (Jackson) and Tom (Cruise).

on the blackboard
making a list of men's names
—all former lovers

In the more advanced afternoon class, I usually challenge these young women to discuss controversial subjects, such as feminism. Today I bring up the subject of *chikan*—men who feel up women, most often in crowded places like subways, where they are helpless to get away. *Chikan* thrive in an overpopulated country where anonymity is prevalent. Molestation proves to be a difficult topic for these nineteen-year-old maidens to talk about. Once I get them started (by making up an imaginary tale of my own), they all have a story to tell.

Most encounters were subtle: an elbow caressing her breast when jostled on the train or a man mashed up against her from behind. But when the man began rubbing up against her, visibly excited, or the anonymous hand ventured up under her skirt— when the motive became clear—then it became "uncomfortable." We talk about the emotions they experienced: surprise, fear, embarrassment, anger. They felt all of these, yet not one woman confronted her molester. Culturally, I understand that it's very hard for them to talk to a man in this situation, but I'm exasperated by their quiet acceptance of these despicable acts.

I end the class by saying, "Isn't it time, ladies, that we speak out and embarrass the men, who are really the ones who should be punished?" Some nod, some hang their heads in yet more embarrassment.

the words *molester*
obscene phone call, pervert
left on the blackboard

Rendezvous

I'm sitting in a restaurant called Tabana ("Taverna") near the Sanjō-Keihan train station having a quick lunch before going to my flower arrangement class. I amuse myself by watching the activity at the busy intersection: teen-age couples wearing matching t-shirts; a group of high-school boys smoking; old people clinging to one other; office ladies carrying handbags one-third their size; salarymen in gray suits; and then a woman who stands out. She shuffles into the square in *geta* sandals. Dressed in a soft pink kimono, her hair is permed and lacquered into place so even the wind can't disturb its symmetry. I watch her tentative movements as she looks for a place to wait where she'll be inconspicuous. She stands near the bus stop, looking demure, aware that she is different from the masses that file by without seeing her. Maybe she feels my eyes on her, staring out the window as I eat my lunch at this pseudo-Greek cafe.

> still as a statue
> hands clasped together
> who's she waiting for?

I decide it's a woman friend and they're going to a cultural event, like a woodblock exhibition or maybe even a Noh play. By the way she moves, I can see that she's comfortable in a kimono. When I've finished my lunch, I notice she's moved to the top of the stairs by the train exit. She stands self-consciously, unwittingly obstructing the crowds which part and flow past her on both sides. Though she doesn't fidget, her face shows shades of doubt and apprehension—no anger, even though she's waited at least twenty minutes for her friend.

The crowds are making me dizzy. I amuse myself by looking for someone I might know. Momentarily distracted, I almost miss the slight flash of pink as the woman turns to meet the person she's been waiting for.

I am not prepared for the handsome, middle-aged man who steps out from the train exit—European-style suit, wavy black hair, immaculately groomed. He hands her flowers wrapped in florist paper and embraces her with his eyes. This is not husband and wife. There's a shyness that disqualifies marriage, an underlying tension, even awkwardness, as they turn toward the street to hail a taxi. A bus obscures my vision, but as it pulls away, I'm reassured to see them standing side by side. This couple would never take a bus. As he scans the busy street to hail a taxi, she peers into the paper wrapping to see what kind of flower he has given her.

> turning away
> she adjusts her *obi*
> one red rose

When he returns to her side with a taxi, she is completely self-possessed. She slides in first. From the window, I can see her smile of anticipation and his, too, just before he bends to get in. The taxi eases away from the crowd. I want to rush down to the street, hail a taxi and say "Follow them!" To see where they go next, to watch the unfolding drama of this rendezvous.

Instead, I board the train for my *ikebana* lesson. Three hours later, I return to Sanjō Street and exit at the same station with my plastic carrying bag of today's flowers. A blond Western woman in a crowd of dark-haired Japanese, I imagine someone looking at me from the restaurant. Pulling back my shoulders, I walk more slowly.

> lingering at the spot
> where the lovers met—
> my wilted roses

Gaijin Gardening

*B*efore John and I find our house in northeast Kyōto, we're offered an opportunity to housesit for an American woman spending the summer in Paris. Her house is situated on a hill at the end of a winding road in the small village of Ishitsukuri-machi. Sandy not only leaves us her quaint farmhouse and teaching jobs, but also an abundance of vegetables from her garden. The cucumbers and zucchini are a foot long—too obscene to give away to anyone.

The neighboring Japanese farmers have even larger gardens, with handmade bamboo fences for their climbing plants. The rows in their vegetable patches are all neat and tidy. I like the wild tangle of eggplants, squash, and tomatoes—not to mention the mysterious Japanese vegetables.

> among the weeds
> a familiar plant—
> marijuana

Our full teaching schedules limit our gardening to Sundays. One hot August afternoon as John and I struggle to tie up the unruly tomato plants, I notice that we have an audience: Mom, Dad, Bro, and Sis standing in a line at the edge of the field. They're all dressed in white outfits appropriate for a summer outing, topped off by straw hats for Mom and Sis and baseball caps for the guys. What a shock it must be for this Japanese family to drive into the "wilderness" only to find *gaijin* at the end of the road. And *gaijin* not relaxing on the porch sipping lemonade, but toiling in a garden.

Dad has a camera with a telephoto lens that makes me wonder exactly what he's zooming in on. True, we do look a bit strange. For one thing, I'm dressed in *mompei*, the indigo-dyed baggy pants that Japanese farmwomen wear, topped off by a conical straw hat. John is barechested, wearing shredded cutoffs and a red L. L. Bean bandana tied around his head. With his red beard, he resembles a half-naked pirate.

> these *gaijin*
> look nothing like
> the ones on Dynasty

John and I ignore them, but they don't go away. Mom and Sis bend down occasionally to pick a flower ("enjoying the nature"), but there's no doubt about it, we are the main attraction. They watch our every move: how we stake up the tomatoes, how we pull weeds, how we speak English so effortlessly.

> *Get a life!* I yell
> they smile and shoot us
> the peace sign

We are fed up with being their Sunday afternoon entertainment. Hot and irritated, I try to figure out how we can get rid of them. Looking around the garden, I pick the largest zucchini I can find and hand it to John. When he sees the smile on my face, he knows exactly what to do.

> standing erect
> in the summer heat—
> *gaijin* gardeners

At the *Sentō*

Naked, carrying a plastic tub and towel
I slide open the inner door to a roomful of
fat women, thin women, young and old women,
all women with black hair and Oriental skin.
They stare at me without looking.

Without speaking, they all decide
I am of the same species—breasts
buttocks, belly button—and go back
to scrubbing themselves with Kao soap,
the brand with a cow on the wrapper.

It's always like this being the outsider.
It doesn't help that my body *is* different
long limbs, blond hair, hairless legs.
And because I have come alone,
I am both suspect and pitiful.
Filling my tub with water
from the spigots—red for hot
blue for cold—I splash it on the tiled
floor before kneeling to wash.
They nod and smile
a good beginning.

Through the slish and slosh and glug of water
I line up soap, shampoo, and creme rinse.

They look/don't look, talk to one another
about the foreign labels and smells and how
I wash my body before my hair.

Theirs is an exclusive club—
women who have grown up,
married, and birthed together.
Scrubbing each other's backs,
they exchange gossip languid as steam.

I knot a towel around my hair
and step into one of the steaming tubs.
Again they look/don't look, hoping
to see me enter the *denki furo*,
the electric-charged tub. But I know
the lightning bolt label, just as I know
the vent in the jacuzzi that sucks up
buttocks. Alone in the tub, I stretch
out, neck on the rim, red toenails
poking up through bubbles.

Then, I cross the room without
holding a washcloth over my pubes,
and sit in the sauna next to a woman
wrapped in tinfoil—sweat inducer.
We watch the hourglass funnel its sand,
imagine pounds dripping off
midriffs, hips, buttocks.

The washing area has filled up now.
Someone has moved my shampoo
to make room for her own:
Kanebo "for beautiful human life."

She is somewhere on the continuum
of scrub, soak, sauna, wash.

I lather up one last time,
rinse my washcloth
under steaming water,
and wring it out tightly
as I have seen them do.
Streams of red dye
run out from between my legs
into the gutter.
The women look, don't look.
All around me the water goes
slish, slosh, and glug.

Newsflash

*E*lderly gentleman poet of Kyōto gets caught with paint thinner under his bed!

His wife, American poet Edith Shiffert, remarked on a peculiar smell one morning as they were having their breakfast.

"What's that awful smell? It's giving me a migraine."

Minoru Sawano tiptoed into his room and, just as he had suspected, the bottle with the paint thinner had toppled over

and leaked into the rug. Through various pantomimes (neither speaks the other's language), the mystery was revealed.

When asked why in heaven's name (or the equivalent in pantomime) he had a bottle of paint thinner under his bed, Minoru dutifully picked up the bottle and carried it to the kitchen. Unscrewing the cap carefully to keep the fumes away from his beloved, he poured the vile liquid down the drain. It took some time before Edith understood that using paint thinner as a germ killer was a time-honored secret of the Sawano family. The chemical and hallucinatory properties of this household helper were unknown in the early Shōwa period. Paint thinner was good enough for him, a traditional man unaware of more modern products such as Sanihousu and Shatto for kitchen and toilet germs, which one can buy at Izumiya, the local department store.

The apartment was opened to air out the noxious fumes. Each poet sat on their respective balconies, bundled in sweaters and heavy socks, not speaking for the remainder of the afternoon.

> the cat Marga
> dozes neutrally
> on the living room sofa

Koha, the Sacred Horse

Tōshōgu Shrine

So sacred, it seems, that he's invisible. But we visit his honorable stable because it's next to the building with the three monkeys. Not actual monkeys or even sacred monkeys, but the famous "see no evil, hear no evil, speak no evil" monkeys. They are carved in paulownia wood on the outside of the building, just under the roof. Charming, playful, but monkeys with a message. Jataka tales, like Aesop's fables, always have a moral for the common folk. They are visual and easy for people to understand.

Koha the Sacred Horse is better understood when we see his schedule. He, like royalty of any kingdom, is a very busy regent. His daily schedule is posted outside his stable:

6 a.m.	fodder (breakfast)
8–9 a.m.	exercise
10–12 noon	service at the stable
noon	fodder (lunch)
2–3 p.m.	exercise, pasturing
4:30 p.m.	fodder (supper)
9:00 p.m.	fodder (dinner)

It's after 2:00 p.m., which means that he is exercising and pasturing. We have unfortunately missed his service at the stable, whatever that is. Perhaps giving rides to members of the samurai class. Or to patrons who have donated millions of yen to gold leaf the doves and dragons on the ceilings of Tōshōgu Shrine. Or, dare we say, to transfer his genes into a filly, prearranged by a *nakōdo* of course. At any rate, he is occupied with other matters. So we, who have traveled across the ocean, are left to imagine his radiant coat, sublime whinny, and majestic gait.

> Koha the Sacred Horse—
> in his royal stall
> only the smell

The Monk of Amida-ji

The pool beneath the waterfall at Amida-ji is deep where the ground has been worn away by incessant dripping, the basin smooth and concave as a freshly-kilned bowl.

> sitting by the stream
> I stop myself
> from weeding the moss

A large orange bee buzzes around me. Is this the spirit of Tanzei Shonin who shut himself in a cave three hundred years ago? Did he, too, linger on these rocks to watch moss grow and ferns cascade down the hillside?

> I hear his voice still
> the monk of Amida-ji
> chanting from the stream

Approaching the entrance to the cave, I am drawn to a portrait of the monk. Wide calm lips, eyes half closed with overhanging eyelids, head shaved, a shadow of eyebrows. I have an uncanny feeling that I've seen him before.

> family album
> bald pate, smooth skin
> my grandfather's face

The cave is dark and wet, water trickling from the moss. This is where Tanzei Shonin spent his last days meditating and chanting, existing only on berries and water. It is said that when the chanting stopped, the caretaker rolled back the stone at the cave's entrance. There he found the monk slumped in a corner, blissfully reposed. His body had become mummified—complete, whole, with no trace of decay.

> sunlight on tatami
> the old Buddhist temple
> smells of candle wax

Well of Beauty

*I*t's a dark place, this Well of Beauty, tucked into a corner of the Zuishin Temple grounds. Each morning the ninth-century *waka* poet, Ono no Komachi, would gaze at her reflection, then bathe her face in the healing waters from Cow Tail Mountain. Its distant flow tempered the chill—unlike her bitter heart. Entranced by her beauty, admirers would come, one after another, to her cottage gate begging for admittance. Her most famous suitor, Prince Fukakusa, is said to have courted her for ninety-

eight days. On the ninety-ninth, the day before she promised to receive him, he fell ill and died in a snowstorm.

The legend of Prince Fukakusa is reenacted every year on the last Sunday in March, with young maidens performing the Hanezu dance. "Hanezu" refers to the deep pink color of the plums blossoming on the temple grounds, a promise of spring.

I feel the darkness of Ono no Komachi's heart as I descend the spiral of stones leading to the now-turbid water in her Well of Beauty—imagine leeches clinging to her milky white skin, ghost lovers entering the cavity of her heart.

> from the mountain forest
> I hear the cuckoo's call
> its blood-red tongue

To Market, To Market

Myong Hee, my Korean friend, comes by at 9:00. We load the car with Balinese sarongs, woodcarvings, baskets, silver jewelry, shell plant hangers, embroidered purses, Christmas ornaments—all purchased on my trips to Thailand, Bali, and the Philippines. Myong Hee has only one item, Korean silk slippers, but she must have two hundred pairs in all sizes and colors. We are headed for the Kitano open-air market, held on the twenty-fifth of every month, to sell our wares.

Kitano Jinja is the Shinto shrine dedicated to the courtier/poet Sugawara Michizane (845–903). After gaining favor in Emperor Uda's court, Michizane became a threat to the powerful Fujiwara clan and they exiled him to Kyūshū. Following his death, plague and drought spread throughout the city, and the Imperial Palace was struck repeatedly by lightning. Kitano Jinja was built to appease his spirit and, years later, he was deified as Tenjin-sama (god of scholarship).

> first plum blossom
> at Kitano Shrine
> spirit of Michizane

Plum blossoms are not what we smell as we make our way along the narrow lanes. Myong Hee and I laugh when we get stuck behind a "honey dipper," a truck that pumps out the toilets of traditional Japanese houses—like ours. Myong Hee tells me that to dream about shit means good fortune. Though this is not a dream, we take it as a propitious sign.

By the time we arrive, the regular vendors are all in place. We find an empty spot near the coffee shop, but there are some problems because we didn't register ahead. A young man takes us to the official's tent.

> five thousand yen
> buys us a spot—
> stench of toilets

It's turning out to be a shitty day. But we're happy to be official—and we're right at the crossroads, in the sunshine and, of course, conveniently close to the toilet. During the day, many friends pass by, surprised to see us selling here instead of buying. Two of my students from Doshisha University stroll by with their mothers. "Chula Sensei!" they shriek. I'm embarrassed, but figure what the hell, it adds to my mystique. Three shabby Japanese musicians linger to chat and ask if I have any Balinese flutes.

> salvaging the butts
> of my clove cigarettes—
> red lipstick stains

The hours pass quickly. Myong Hee and I talk, laugh, drink coffee from a thermos and eat the bean cakes that our neighbor sends over. The punk guy next to us want to trade one of his cheap pens for a fish ornament. I bargain with him and get a wool dress for two fish. It's all so different when you're part of the organization, even though we know it's run by the yakuza, the Japanese mafia. Yvonne comes by wearing a photo of her Indian guru Rajneesh around her neck. She tells me that her friends two stalls down are selling Indian imports. I buy sandalwood incense from them and light a few sticks. The toilet stench is scaring away customers. Eileen, the *Village Voice* critic I met in Bali, is trying on glass bracelets from India and has already broken one.

At 4:00, the sun disappears and it gets cold. Sellers begin to pack up, loading antiques, kimonos, plants, children's toys, shoes, and food into their trucks that appear out of nowhere.

> stomachs full of bean cakes
> pockets full of yen—home again
> home again, jiggety-jig

Firefly Lanterns *(Hotaru Bukuro)*

*I*n early June, we get a telephone call from Murayama-san, our potter friend from Ayabe.

"Meg-gie," he says, "the fireflies are out!"

"Okay," I say, "we'll be right up!"

Ayabe is a two-and-a-half hour drive from Kyōto along a rural highway that meanders through mountain villages. John and I pack an overnight bag and leave right after our university classes finish. Murayama-san, his wife, Ayako, and ten-year-old daughter, Tomoko, greet us warmly outside their old farmhouse. Though we are the best of friends, we call him by his surname. So does his wife.

Ayako prepares a simple meal of tofu, fish, and vegetables from her garden. As soon as it gets dark, we gather nets and glass jars and head outside. It's a remarkably clear night for *tsuyu*.

> stars, stars' reflections
> mirrored in the paddy field
> oh! the fireflies

They land on the grasses bordering the rice fields and on the *hotaru bukuro*, white bellflowers, that thrive in the damp soil. Tomoko plucks a bellflower for me and explains that *hotaru* means firefly and *bukuro* is sack. With our butterfly nets, we scoop the air and capture a net full of fireflies. Carefully we transfer them to the *hotaru bukuro* by opening the blossoms and inserting the fireflies into their petal-soft cage. Soon the flowers begin to take on the glow of the fireflies' light. By the end of an hour, we have a handful of lanterns to guide our way home. Other fireflies are contained in jars. How many do we have? Fifty? One hundred? It's impossible to count them with their lights flickering on and off, on and off.

At the farmhouse we remove our shoes and gather in the main room, settling down on the tatami. Murayama-san goes outside to his kiln and selects some small cups from a recent firing. He presents each of us with a pristine cup and fills it with *sake*.

Kampai! he toasts.

Kampai! we echo, raising the smooth cups to our lips.

Our host closes all the *fusuma* to the rest of the house then, opening the lids on the glass jars, he releases the fireflies into the room. Tomoko and I peel back the petals of the *hotaru bukuro* and coax our captives from their silken cages. They dart and flick, flash their green lights as they settle on arms and knees, and on the Japanese scroll in the alcove.

> lying on tatami
> in a room full of fireflies
> the evening cool

In the darkened room, we drink *sake* and talk softly, speak of gentle things, the importance of friendship, the natural abundance of life. For hours, we lie on the tatami whispering, as night deepens and the *sake* bottle empties. On the ceiling, the stars flicker on and off, on and off. When it's finally time to retire, Murayama-san opens the *shōji* and releases the fireflies into the night. By morning they will have scattered far and wide, specks of darkness against the overcast sky.

Namu Amida Butsu

Sanzen-in Temple

Chanting
in the gray afternoon
between summer and autumn
wreathed vowels
avowals of young monks
heads thatched like Ōhara roofs
against the winter.

Prayer beads in Buddha hands
long, tapering lotus stems
strike the wooden fish.
Muffled, the beat,
like a skull stuffed
with damp rags.

Nothing moves but lips and gong
air heavy with the hum
of dying cicadas
Namu Amida Butsu
  Namu Amida Butsu
    Namu Amida Butsu

I'm inside
a chest of cedar
child small
knees to forehead.
My hands clasp
a sandalwood *mala*.

Prayers curl
into each other
like rings of smoke.

Spiraling through the keyhole
into the smoky dusk,
they hover
over the pond
and color the fish
saffron.

The Crow's Call

at the mountain shrine
a nun claps her hands
caw! caw!

At home we argue about how many times that crow cawed. John says only once; I say twice. I check to make sure we at least heard this at the same time—and we did. "If we had a third person with us, then he would verify it," I say. But if there was a third person, we'd probably have been talking and wouldn't have heard anything. I prefer to be quiet in the woods.

Living in another culture where everything is new and different exacerbates our differences. More and more, we're living separate realities, with John's always being the "real" one. When I say "I'd swear on my grandmother's grave that I heard two crow calls," he says: "Your grandmother would rise up and say John's right. That John is a smart boy!" I laugh, but then I'm angry. Trying to alienate even my grandmother from me. Worse yet, I'm beginning to believe that I am becoming the mad woman that everyone tries to humor, the woman whose reality is surreal, but unthreatening, for the time being anyway. And I remember New Year's Eve, ringing the bell to rid the world of sin— feeling wonderfully cleansed. As we descended the stairs, I looked up at the trees and exclaimed, "Oh, look plum blossoms!" John immediately corrected me saying they were reflections of electric lights. Then I heard a voice saying, "If Maggie sees plum blossoms, then they're plum blossoms. Let her see them!" It was our friend Reinier and I blessed him.

It's a beautiful autumn day and we are enjoying our drive up to Ōhara, through the mountain villages north of Kyōto. I catch my breath, however, when John turns off on the very dirt road where I drove on Thursday to get away and be alone. And then he parks in the same spot I did. Needing to gather my thoughts, I find a rough-edged stone and began to cut pampas grass with it.

> sawing, sawing
> the pampas stalks
> red as blood

We head up a narrow road behind two men in white plastic boots. When we ask what they're looking for they say *"chabana"* (flowers for tea ceremony), but won't tell us the name of the plant. Passing under the orange *torii* gate, we enter a mountain shrine. It's strange to hike in places where we can't read any of the signs, which are written in *kanji*. Up, up through the woods, dark greens broken by bursts of reds and yellows, and the late afternoon light illuminating the moss on the stone steps.

Finally the ascent levels off to a wide path, fallen leaves smooth underfoot as we wipe our brows and take off sweaters. Passing through another *torii*, we come upon a wayside shrine with a termite-eaten donation box. I take it down and look inside. It has only a few one-yen coins that no one will ever use. Inside the small enclosure are two faces carved in stone; they look like Okina, the old man in a Noh play. Then I notice the chrysanthemums.

> strewn along the path
> chrysanthemums
> guiding me where?

Above, maples turning red swirl like umbrellas, shadowing the clearing, which has been recently swept. Suddenly, in the middle of a forest, we come upon a bamboo gate. After some hesitation, I climb over it. An old nun is facing an altar, her hands grasping a rope to ring a bell to call the gods. She claps her hands twice in prayer. Just at that moment, a crow caws twice. I laugh at the coincidence. The nun looks over at me, a blond foreign woman. Incense smoke swirls up and around and behind her, making her look like an apparition. The smell of incense is very strong.

"May I come forward?" I greet her in Japanese.

"Are you only one?" she asks.

I look behind me and answer, "No, a couple."

"No, you cannot come," she says emphatically.

Embarrassed and disappointed, I gesture to the forest and say *"Kirei!"* Beautiful.

As I climb back over the gate, I wonder if I could find this shrine again. Something has drawn me to this place, to this solitary nun in the forest wearing a white scarf over her head. And then I remember a story I wrote about a woman running away to the mountains and living alone in a temple. Could this be Yukiko? As I walk away, I identify the vegetables in her small garden: *daikon, gobo,* beans strung up on a pole and, of course, chrysanthemums to place on the altar.

> in the silence
> a crow caws
> calling me home

Dream of Ablutions

I'm inside a building that looks like a mausoleum: high ceilings, walls spackled with mauve, and marble pillars supporting the structure. Along the walls are stations—not the Roman Catholic Stations of the Cross, but more like alcoves in a beauty salon. A kind of religious spa. Workers in white uniforms bustle around complaining about how tired they are from washing feet, giving back rubs, and cleaning up after the "seekers."

This is all hype, I say to no one in particular. A woman in line turns around and gives me a dirty look. I separate myself from the devotees and make my way to the center of an empty room. Floor patterns radiate in all directions, like a mandala. There are many doors, all half-size so you have to stoop to enter. I kneel down to open one and find myself face to face with a young Buddhist monk. He's as startled as I am.

With a steady gaze, he hands me a bucket of water and bows his head, indicating that I'm to pour it over his shaven pate. After I give him ablutions, he hands me a white towel sculpted into the shape of a mask. Not knowing what to do, I place it over his face. In the distance, uproarious laughter from the older monks. My black-robed monk sits unperturbed with the towel on his head. Then, suddenly, he whips it off and kisses me. Come back here at 2:00 a.m., he whispers.

> the next morning
> sitting meditation
> with a smile

Early Chill

in the classroom
the smell of mothballs
early chill

Driving home from a long day of teaching, I begin to bicker with John. To make matters worse, we're stuck in a traffic jam. Through the car window, we watch Japanese sweeping the sidewalks in front of their houses or their shops. They use small, short brooms, which are not at all up to the task. All around them, ginkgo leaves flutter down. We watch their frenzied sweeping and burst out laughing.

sweeping, sweeping, sweep—
the old woman's broom
no match for the wind

At home, I too get carried away and begin to sweep leaves from our moss garden. This is a delicate task, removing leaves without disturbing the moss. My broom is made from branches of bamboo and has a bamboo handle. It's a work of art. Best of all, the handle is long enough so even a tall foreigner like myself doesn't have to stoop. All the patterns of leaves, burrs, and bare branches inspire me to do a flower arrangement. When I finish sweeping, I scour the yards of the deserted houses on Gaijin Mura (Foreigners' Village) for materials. My greatest find is a huge fan-shaped leaf with a cicada shell still clinging to the underside. Dry and dusty, it still holds the shape of the cicada it has protected. It saddens me to realize that, with the arrival of autumn, the cicada too will be dead.

> clinging to a leaf
> the husk of a cicada
> becomes *ikebana*

Why is it that we never find their bodies? Do they burrow under the earth to lay eggs in autumn and then die already buried?

> nine years to be born
> yet cicadas sing fully
> through only one season

Just before sunset, I take a walk on a path behind our house. Sheaves of rice hang upside down, drying from bamboo racks. Soon the farm women will gather to thresh rice onto woven mats, then store it in bags for the winter. At the end of the path, I linger beneath the persimmon tree. I remember a Japanese friend telling me about the custom of not picking a tree bare during the harvest. Something is always left to feed the passing traveler or the birds. In the animist Shinto tradition, the last fruit on the tree is left as an offering so next year's harvest will be bountiful.

> the sun sets
> behind winter trees
> last persimmon

Fallen Persimmon Hut (Rakushisha)

November, late afternoon. The sun sets behind Mt. Ogurayama in western Kyōto. A narrow road winds up through the valley, passing through the village of Sagano with its picturesque thatched-roofed houses. As we walk up the lane to Mukai Kyorai's Fallen Persimmon Hut, a cold wind begins to blow through the bamboo leaves—*sasa, sasa*.

> the cuckoo
> through the dense bamboo grove
> moonlight seeping
> —Matsuo Bashō

Kyorai, Bashō's most talented disciple, continued his master's haiku style after he died. Bashō visited Rakushisha several times, including a month there in 1752 where he completed the *Saga Diary*. In a corner of the garden stands a poem stone with the haiku that Bashō ended his diary with:

> summer rains
> trace of a poem card
> torn off the wall
> —Matsuo Bashō

Rakushisha is enclosed by a high hedge, separating it from the rice fields outside. The crop has recently been harvested, leaving only stubble.

fallen rice kernels
the crows call loudly
sway of bamboo

The name "Fallen Persimmon Hut" comes from an incident in Kyorai's life. In the garden, he had a large grove of about forty persimmon trees. One autumn day, when they were heavy with fruit, he arranged to sell them to a Kyōto merchant for a good price. But, the night before they were to be picked, a great storm arose. He could hear persimmons rattling on the roof as they fell and smashed on the ground. The next morning, not a single persimmon was left on the trees. For Kyorai, this was a *satori* experience: fate had intervened to teach him about attachment to worldly desires.

at Kyorai's hut
a bashō tree
among the persimmons

On the outside wall of the hut, Kyorai has placed a poem box for poets to leave their haiku. I peer into the crack. It's empty. Three hundred years later, there are still signs of him. His sandals and conical straw hat and raincoat hang on the outside wall to indicate that he's at home. I write this haiku and put it in the mailbox:

> the poet's *geta*
> still at the entryway
> autumn chill

At Rakushisha, there's a sense of continuity—of keeping the poetic spirit alive. The monk poet Saigyō (1118–1190) lived here in seclusion before Kyorai. His well is preserved in a corner of the garden. Bashō was Kyorai's teacher; the poet Chomu respected his master Kyorai; and modern-day Shaku Hyosai, a journalist for the *Asahi Newspaper* and an accomplished practitioner of *haiga*, has continued to preserve Rakushisa as a sanctuary.

> left behind—
> the autumn wind
> a single gravestone

Kyorai's gravestone lies in the Kōgen-ji graveyard, about 100 meters north of Rakushisha. In keeping with his humility, it's a small stone marked simply with "Kyorai."

> Fallen Persimmon Hut
> ripe persimmons hang heavy
> over my head

Shinju-an, The Pearl Hermitage

*I*kkyū, the free-spirited Zen priest and poet, lived in this subtemple of Daitoku-ji. In the main room, you can view a wooden image of him, complete with his actual beard and hair cuttings attached. This is interesting as all paintings show him with a shaved head. According to our guide, the framed *kanji* above the image says: "This image resembles me greatly, don't you think?"

> in a dark recess
> Ikkyū in shadow
> bright chrysanthemums

The East Garden was designed by Murata Jukō, founder of the tea ceremony. Jukō practiced Zen meditation under the guidance of Ikkyū. His garden is an abstraction of nature, with rocks grouped to represent islands or mountains.

> azalea cluster
> the size of my hand
> for a hundred years

As in any dry stone garden, the meaning is in the mind of the beholder. Looking at the stones arranged in 7-5-3 groupings with a background of green moss, I feel obliged to write a 7-5-3 haiku.

> view hidden by bamboo now
> where is Mt. Hiei
> three stones high

As an afterthought, our guide shows us the Well of Pure Water where *The Tale of Genji* author, Murasaki Shikibu, was bathed as a newborn.

> my face reflected
> in a thousand-year-old well
> scabs of lichen

From the veranda, we look out over the graves of head priests from past centuries. I wonder which one is "One Pause" Ikkyū's. For his death poem, he boldly wrote the calligraphy in four vertical lines, but forgot one character, which he added later in the margins.

> writing his final poem
> the uselessness
> of perfection

The Weight of Stones

*A*perfect autumn day in Kyōto. We join a tour of the Sentō
Gosho, the Imperial Palace strolling garden with plants,
water, and stones arranged to give the viewer a surprise at every
turn. Our leader pauses at a beach of smooth stones all the
same size, about four inches in diameter. They were gathered in
Odawara in eastern Japan, he tells us, and individually wrapped
in silk before being transported to Kyōto and presented to the
Emperor. They're called "two-liter stones," for each was said to
be worth two liters of rice at that time.

I stand on the pathway at the edge of the pond counting the stones
to get some sense of their worth. After one hundred, I give up. I
want to pick one up, to feel its coldness in my palm and the veneer
of six centuries of weather. I want to find the soul of this stone and,
holding it, know that the cost of just one would feed a Japanese
family for days. I want to hear about the peasants who died of
hunger as they tithed their *daimyō*, who courted the Emperor's
favor by offering these stones. And I want to understand a culture
that values the beauty of stones over human lives.

> new-age fad
> the well-polished surface
> of worry stones

Hexed

*L*ast week I got a chain letter in the mail.

> This letter has been around the world ten times. Upon receiving it, you must make twenty copies and send it out to ten people within ninety-six hours. After a period of three to four days, good luck will come to you. If you do NOT send copies of this letter, death, tragedy, and misfortune will befall you.

> Laura Keen, a model in Los Angeles, refused to forward copies of this letter. Four days after receiving it, she tripped on a root in the sidewalk, breaking her leg and chipping her two front teeth.

> James Sheldon forgot to send copies of this letter and was stung to death by a hive of killer bees.

> Harold Tompkins plummeted to his death in a small aircraft he was piloting. A copy of this letter was found in the pocket of his flight jacket.

> These, folks, were no accidents! Send your letters today!!!

No way was I going to send this pox to any of my friends. But what to do with it? Throwing it in the trash would not exorcise its evil. I only had ninety-six hours, four days, and guess what day that fell on. Friday the thirteenth. There was only one thing to do—burn the sucker.

Clearing a spot in the dirt lane in front of our house, I lit three sticks of incense and arranged them in a triangle. Then, I crumpled the letter and its envelope and placed them inside the triangle. It took several matches to ignite them. When they started to burn, I made the sign of the cross and chanted like a Buddhist priest:

> Fire, take away the evil from this paper.
> All evil is burning away, burning away.
> This is the end of the chain
> and any evil it may cause.

The letter and envelope popped and crackled as they burnt.

> my husband walks by—
> tosses his soiled Kleenex
> into the fire

Nezumi Jet Coaster

tree limb shadows
blow across the *shōji*
mice in the closet

One autumn evening while looking for a vase in the hallway, I lifted out a roll of *washi* paper stored behind the bureau. Out flew seven baby mice! They skittered down into the *genkon* and behind the shoe rack. John was vacuuming in the next room with our old-fashioned canister vacuum cleaner. When he heard my shrieks, he pulled the vacuum down into the entryway and sucked them up. SLURRRP!! Then he unplugged the vacuum, detached the hose, and carried the canister outside.

"Did you kill them?" I asked when he returned.

He smiled.

"What did you do with them?"

"Those baby mice sure are good swimmers," he replied. He had dumped them into the irrigation stream at the end of the road.

Mama got away. She was still somewhere in the house.

The next day I told this story to my students at Kyōto Seika College. One girl looked as though she was going to cry. *"Kawaii so, nezumi-*

chan!" (poor baby mice) she wailed. In the back row, a young man yelled out, "Happy! Jet coaster!" laughing as he imagined the mice having a roller coaster ride through the vacuum hose. So now John and I call the vacuum cleaner the *Nezumi* Jet Coaster.

Mama surfaced a few nights later, darting out from the closet where we hid our TV. It is also the closet with our diaries, books, and photographs, so we were eager to flush her out, especially since she would probably build another nest there. For two nights, John lay in wait with the vacuum hose aimed at the TV. Finally, after no sign of the mouse, he began dragging everything out of the closet.

"I'll find that mouse if it's the last thing I do here!" We were leaving Japan for good in three months.

> recycling pile
> a foot high
> no mouse

"Where could she have gone to?" John said, exasperated.

"She's probably in that closet now," I said, pointing to the next closet that needed to be cleaned.

A Gathering of Souls

I'm thinking of burying Henry tomorrow. It will be hard to part from him—we've been together for over ten years on two continents—but Henry hasn't been the same since the fire. Though he survived the temple fire in Kyōto without mishap, he didn't fare as well in Oregon. Last summer's house fire scarred his face and left permanent marks on his once-perfect skin. His clothing, too, has taken on a dusty pallor. Once immaculate and debonair in a brown kimono with a sandalwood fan tucked into his *haori*, he now looks somewhat shabby. Nevertheless, he is still a treasure.

I first saw Henry at the Dolls Requiem at Hokyo-ji in 1983. This Buddhist temple in north Kyōto was founded in 1360 as a nunnery for the Rinzai sect, with emperors' daughters becoming head nuns. Daughters of the Tokugawa, Keshu, and Mito families brought their dolls here every year on March 3 for *Hina Matsuri*, the Doll Festival. As the collection of dolls grew over the ages, Hokyo-ji became known as Ningyo-dera, the Doll Temple. Ironically, this festival originated from a Chinese purification rite in which evils were transferred onto dolls, which were then cast into the river. No Japanese would consider throwing their precious dolls (many of them works of art) into the river or even into the trash for they believe that dolls, like humans, have souls.

> discarded dolls
> lined up on the altar
> their eyes wide open

Hokyo-ji is the only temple in Kyōto to hold a requiem for dolls. Every October people from the surrounding areas bring shopping bags full of their worn-out dolls to be blessed and then burned. I had also brought a pair of dolls, which had been given to me when I first arrived in Japan. At that time I didn't know that if I admired something, it would be given to me. I cherished these dolls as much for their age as for their beauty. Their pale faces were delicately painted, each eyelash visible, every hair in place in their elaborate coiffures. They had heads that could be turned and hands with tapered fingers and even indentations for nails. Dressed in red silk kimonos laced with gold thread, these *hina* dolls depicted an ideal beauty. My friend, Michiko, once told me that one of her earliest memories was of her father holding her face between his hands and saying "I hope you will become an *echima-san* (princess doll)."

Dolls mark certain rites of passage for Japanese girls. A girl usually receives a set of *hina* dolls at birth or on her fifth birthday and keeps them for her trousseau. Every year around mid-February, these dolls and their entourage of musicians, ministers, and court ladies are taken out of their wooden boxes and displayed on a tiered platform in observance of the Doll Festival. Leaving them out after March 3rd is considered unlucky—the girl may get married late or not at all.

> displaying my doll
> in the alcove year round
> her dusty robes

After adding my two dolls to the makeshift altar in the courtyard, I entered the temple to view the famous collection. The dolls range in size from tiny figurines displayed in showcases to life-size mannequins. Dressed in six layers of kimonos with hair falling below their waists, these exquisite dolls sit poised over the *koto* or with brush raised for calligraphy. Women of the court sit in elegant repose, eyes lowered in a dreamy gaze. In another room the more active dolls, dressed in indigo-dyed clothes and straw hats, stroll across the tatami playing the *biwa* or participate in various courtly ball games. They look so lifelike that it is easy to believe the legends. People believe that they come alive every night and dance, resuming their exact positions at first light.

> behind the glass
> in the display case
> the princess's hair
> still growing

Though there are countless dolls at Hokyo-ji, the most famous by far is Bansein. Favorite plaything of Emperor Gosai-in's daughter, Bansein served three princesses and was treated like a person. She was given her own wardrobe of outfits for all seasons, her own tableware, and a sword. To this day, she seems to hold forth at Hokyo-ji. Locals have reported seeing the dim light of a candle as Bansein does her night watch.

I stepped out into the bright courtyard where a crowd had gathered to unpack their dolls. Some people had wrapped their doll's head in tissue paper so they would be protected from further damage until they were burned. The accumulation of dolls on the altar had grown, nearly dwarfing my two *echima* dolls. And what strange juxtapositions—samurai warriors next to Kewpie dolls, cylindrical wooden *kokeshi* propping up teddy bears, cute stuffed animals nuzzling Edo-period princesses.

> still life
> all the dolls' memories
> huddled together

On a previous visit to Hokyo-ji, I had met the head nun, Sawada Eisai. "Why are these beautiful and rare dolls brought here to be burned when someone else could enjoy them?" I asked. She replied without hesitation. "Each doll has a special reason for being brought here. They are not just old and unwanted. A thoughtless owner could just throw them away, but they were brought here instead. We have to respect the wishes of the donor. If they had wanted to pass the doll along, they would have done so."

I knelt down beside an old woman and watched her unpack her dolls. When she smiled at me, I asked why she had brought her dolls to this ceremony. "I heard from a neighbor at the temple that you could bring your old dolls here," she replied. "I brought many *kokeshi*. I have too many souvenir dolls. They are so heavy that I couldn't bring many, but I'll bring the rest next year." I helped her arrange them on the altar and when we were finished, she handed me her tea ceremony ticket since she had to leave right after the requiem.

> *kokeshi* dolls
> with no arms or legs
> her daughter in a wheelchair

An old man next to us was unloading a boxful of *hina* dolls. "These dolls are old and I couldn't give them away," he said. "They have soul, so I brought them here. It is the custom for people who have been living here for a long time to bring their dolls to Ningyo-dera. I've been coming for five years."

It was then that I saw Henry. He was leaning toward a young girl with the most beautiful porcelain skin. When I looked closely, I realized that they were twins, dressed in similar kimonos from another age. But it was not his elegant bearing I was drawn to—it was the expression of utter tranquility on his face. He seemed removed from the others, and I wondered what circumstances had brought him here.

at the temple
love at first sight
what a doll!

A middle-aged woman who had overheard my conversation with the others stooped down next to me and took out blue-eyed dolls and *hina* dolls and stuffed animals. "These were my daughter's," she said stroking the doll's hair. "She died when she was a child. She was very beautiful, like an *echima* doll. I kept all her dolls to remind me of her. I've had them so many years. My second daughter now has children and I have grandchildren. These dolls of my first daughter are getting old, so I decided to bring them here." I admired each one as she placed them respectfully on the altar.

> walking away with
> her empty shopping bag
> "Kanebo For Beautiful Life"

A bell rang to announce the beginning of the requiem ceremony. Sawada Eisai, emerged from the temple with her entourage of nuns and priests. She had aged since I'd last seen her, back bent with a dowager's hump, but her face was pure as a girl's. Sawada-sama had lived her whole life in the temple among these dolls. With her shaved head and splendid gold and purple robes, she looked like a doll herself. As she offered up prayers for the souls of *hina* and Kewpie dolls alike, her voice began to crack. Elderly people stood at rapt attention throughout the ceremony, imagining the souls of their dolls rising up on spirals of incense. I looked over at Henry, who was staring straight ahead unblinking, hands relaxed by his side.

In closing, Sawada-sama recited a poem by Saneatsu Mushakōji:

Dear Dolls,

People who made you
who loved you
you will never know,
but because you were loved
you will die peacefully.

People quietly said a last good-bye to their cherished dolls as the loudspeaker of a recycling truck blared outside the temple walls.

After everybody bustled out, I stayed to help load the dolls into boxes and transport them to a storeroom at the back of the temple. Now soulless, the dolls were mere objects. I was surprised to see how they were just crammed into boxes. In a few days, they would be burned on a funeral pyre. As I worked, I kept an eye out for one last glimpse of Henry, but he had disappeared.

Then, as I delivered my last load, I spotted him. His delicate body had been jammed between a furry orange tiger and a teddy bear. But at least he was on top of the pile. His twin sister was nowhere to be seen. It was a sign, I told myself.

without a second thought
I tuck Henry inside
the folds of my cape

Faint Profiles

$\mathcal{A}$lthough I've visited Hōsen-in Temple countless times in every season, I've never taken a photo of the garden—not even the famous "Ceiling of Blood." These wood ceiling panels, once the floorboards of Fushimi Castle, now hold outlines of samurai who committed *hara-kiri* after being defeated by their enemies. Japanese come here to view their bloody profiles. I come to Hōsen-in to listen to wind in the bamboo. Bamboo that sounds like a snake in one season, a dragonfly in another. To listen to water spilling into a stone urn from a bamboo pole. To view the six-hundred-year-old pine tree shaped to look like Mt. Fuji. And to enjoy the seasonal delights, like watching the snow fall while drinking green tea and warming my hands over the porcelain *hibachi*.

> *hibachi* embers
> red berries
> dusted with snow

One of the pleasures of village temples is a visit to the toilet. *Sabi*, the Japanese aesthetic of rustic simplicity, is in evidence here. The booth is constructed of cedar grown in the nearby forests. Nesting in a basket on the floor, a ream of toilet paper, thin as picnic napkins, weighted down by a river-polished stone. The wooden toilet cover is handmade. How many years of training to create such an artistic toilet seat? Through the half-open window, you can see the mountains and forests of Ōhara. A spray of wildflowers, arranged in a narrow vase, graces the wooden shelf built specifically for that purpose.

washing my hands
I bow to the rusty sink
level with my knees

Returning to the main room, I sit on the tatami by a sunny window and jot haiku in my journal. The sun moves deeper into the room as time passes. The wind becomes colder. How quickly summer has gone. I keep expecting it to return any day now.

bamboo leaves drifting
in the mountain wind
dragonflies

To keep warm, I walk around the temple and peer into the back room. The old women are counting stacks of 500-yen bills, calling out numbers, tabulating the temple's profits, and reserving a portion for their old age. Standing in front of a glass door, I notice a reflection of a woman. She's wearing a blue coat, maroon scarf, and a beret. It's a while before I recognize myself. Behind the glass, one of the old women looks up at me, her face superimposed upon mine.

faint profiles
bamboo shadows
my reflection blurs

A Warm Winter's Night

All the way to Maruyama Park, I sit in the back of the bus, huddled in a black wool cape. Something on the bus smells musty, like an iron burning. Did I forget to unplug the iron in my hasty departure? Or is it the smell of the white fur coat of the woman next to me?

> my prize possession
> a black wool *tombi*
> worn by old men

Walking through this famous park, it's hard not to be distracted by the solitary fish in the pond, a duck sitting on a rock next to an empty *sake* bottle, a young couple looking for privacy on a cold bench. But I hurry by, wanting to be punctual for this dinner party hosted by the English department teachers at Ōtani High School. They are my students; we meet once a week to refresh their English by reading a book together. I've been teaching them for over three years and affectionately call them the Ōtani Boys.

This was my first teaching job when I arrived in Japan. All four men were present at the interview, pads and pencils in hand to take notes. Their previous teacher was a missionary named Ford and they had just read *Hedda Gabler* with him. They never imagined hiring a woman teacher as they heard American women were "very independent." Nevertheless, we went over my resume line by line, even my hobbies.

"I have another applicant to interview on Monday," Inoue-san, the head teacher, said when we had finished. "It gives me a headache to choose."

Without thinking I blurted out, "Oh, choose me and then you will have no headache!" Evidently he liked my humor because I was offered the job the next day.

I arrive at Senryu, an exquisitely well-maintained traditional Japanese house, just as the clock bongs 5:00. Sliding open the door, I announce myself by calling out "*Konbanwa*."

Dogs bark and the owners emerge still wearing aprons over their kimonos. The old women bow when they see me, the guest of honor.

> welcoming me
> the proprietors lick rice
> from the corners of their mouths

The first to arrive, I am ushered into the room and seated in front of the kerosene space heater, where they serve me green tea. The conversation is in Japanese and revolves around my outfit: first the *tombi*, then my pink silk *haori* jacket. I hope they won't notice the small tear in the crotch of my pants, and take care to keep my legs folded under me in a ladylike manner. When they ask where I bought these Japanese clothes, I tell them Kitano Temple market. One of the women is wearing an exquisite Nishijin-woven kimono.

> stains on her kimono
> how long before it's sold
> at Kitano market

For fifteen minutes, I respond to their questions in Japanese. "How long have you been in Japan? Are you married? How many children? What do you think about Japan?" I have memorized my responses in Japanese and am fluent in this predictable line of polite conversation. When they say something I don't understand, I smile agreeably. Later I realize they were saying I was "clever" finding such beautiful bargains at Kitano—and there I was nodding and agreeing with them the whole time!

Just as my Japanese begins to falter, the Ōtani Boys arrive, all rosy-cheeked and healthy in wool sweaters and tweed pants. Inoue, Soga, Sakamoto, and Asahino. Asahino-san has known these women, two sisters, since his college days over thirty years ago. They take off their aprons for him.

> excusing myself
> I call my English neighbor
> to check on the iron

It is so relaxed here with the fire burning, the *nabe* pot bubbling on the heater, hot *sake*, and cold beer. "Just like the *sento*," I say to the guys as we change to beer, "first the hot, then the cold." The gaudy gold screens are covered with plastic sheeting, the Japanese dolls encased in glass. We talk in English about the Japanese sense of "group." Do I think Japanese are rich (my necklace falls off at this point), and parking ticket stories, which have us rolling with laughter.

"Remember the first book we read together?" I ask them during a pause.

"Charlotte's Web!" they say in unison, wide smiles on their faces.

"And do you remember how insulted you were when you discovered it was a children's book?"

They all groan and nod. After the first chapter, they were hooked. We spent many pleasant afternoons in that barnyard with Charlotte, Wilbur, and all the animals. And, like children, when we finished the book, they wanted to read it again.

It's after eleven when we finally say our good-byes. I stroll alone through Maruyama Park lit by yellow lights. The ancient cherry trees are bare and braced on wooden crutches for the winter so their branches will not be broken by snowfall.

> stiff limbs
> warmed by *sake*
> winter silence

In the Japan Alps

*C*loudy morning. The snow-covered mountains are no longer visible. I head into the cold wind to investigate the straw-thatched houses I've seen from afar.

> walking north
> the wind blows
> my breath behind me

Each house has a *kura* storehouse with its own family crest written in Chinese script on a plaque over the door. I stop to sketch the building, then continue on, listening to the sound of a stream, the flap of a bird's wings, and

> from afar
> faint tinkle
> of a wind chime

Can it really be a wind chime—so out of place in winter? As I ascend further from the road, I notice that the water in the fields has frozen. Also, there are no animal sounds.

> stacked in the fallow fields
> piles of rice sheaves
> *tanuki* shelters

On these daily walks, I rarely see people or even hear them. It's too cold for Japanese to wander outside like this crazy American. Passing one house, I hear people talking and, feeling lonely, glance through the window

> from outside
> voices around the wood stove
> their drowsy whine

It begins to snow, the flakes invisible on my white coat and hat. I head up a road that ends in a forest of cedars. Suddenly I hear a pecking sound and glimpse a flash of red—a woodpecker, judging from the red breast and black-and-white coloring. I watch him, enthralled, as he pecks insects from bare branches. He keeps flying ahead of me, urging me on.

> stopping to write
> every few feet
> cackle of crows

The snow is coming down harder and the afternoon quickly turning to evening. Time to head back to Miasa Cultural Center and sit under the *kotatsu* with a pot of green tea—or better yet, a flask of *sake*. But which way to go? For a moment, I panic as I imagine the headlines: *American Poet Found Frozen to Death in Japan Alps with Haiku Notebook in Hand.*

> afternoon walk
> my ink freezes
> writing this hai . . .

The Great Hermit Temple

*F*ounded in 1509, Daisen-in is one of the largest temples in the complex of Daitoku-ji. Its east garden is famous for having the first *karesansui*, dry landscape garden. Designed after a Sung-dynasty painting of cliffs and falling water, this garden evokes the spirit of an ink painting with its mountainous landscape, misty valleys, and asymmetrical design. The entire garden, only twelve feet wide and forty-seven feet long, was built around a boat-shaped rock representing Takarabune, the mythical treasure ship piloted by the Seven Lucky Gods. There's a tension of stillness in the rock, surrounded by a river of gravel,

crane- and tortoise-shaped islands, and shrubs. Japanese throng to the bridge to have their photos taken.

> after they leave
> only the wind
> and the incense

When Sen no Rikyū held a tea ceremony in this tearoom more than four hundred years ago for Hideyoshi, the imperial regent of Japan, he placed a *chabana* on this rock. His guests could view the arrangement from the tearoom when they gazed out. In the spirit of Zen, it was very likely a single flower, for the emptiness of rocks and the white gravel would be the main focal point.

I try to imagine which flowers he chose. In spring, perhaps a sprig of plum; in summer, a Rose of Sharon blossom; for autumn, a spray of bush clover, and in winter, a red camellia. The container would also be appropriate to the season: a tall, pastel-colored vase for plum; a container of freshly-cut bamboo in summer; in autumn, a basket woven from reeds or willow to set off the delicacy of bush clover; and, in winter, black lacquer ware to accentuate the camellia.

> touching the rock
> where Rikyū placed flowers
> my fingers trace centuries

Moving to the south side of the *hondō*, I sit on the smooth wood of the *engawa* and meditate on the larger dry stone garden. In the far corner is a single tree, the *sarasōju* grown from a cutting of one of the sal trees under which Buddha passed into *parinirvana*.

four hundred years old
limbs of the *sarasōju*
Buddha's bones

When I view a dry stone garden, I feel as though I'm shedding myself. And yet, there's a feeling of resistance. Nothing moves in the stone garden but an ant. I follow its progress for some time. Before long my notebook comes out to record thoughts that true meditators strive to let go of. But I'm a poet, not a Zen monk.

searching for what
ant in the raked garden
crawling up, crawling down

a sparrow hops
into the waves, then
flies to the other side

When I arrived earlier in the afternoon, the abbot signed my book with his name, my name, and the phrase: "Every day is training." It's a belief to contemplate, to say to oneself each day upon rising, during the day when struggling with difficulty, and just before falling asleep. It will give meaning to our daily lives and guide our dreams at night.

spring wind
stones in the dry garden
flow without moving

Rikyū's Last Tea

Kan-in (Tea Room of Contentment), Kyōto

S en no Rikyū rises early to have a simple meal of *miso* soup and rice with his wife. He dresses in a white undergarment and, over that, dons a black kimono with his family crest. Wrapping a sash round his waist, he puts on white *tabi* and moves to the door where his wife is waiting to say good-bye. They kneel on tatami and bow, honoring their years together, thanking each other for past kindnesses. Rikyū steps down into the entryway and slips into wooden sandals. His wife remains kneeling until he disappears.

In the garden, a light snow is falling. Rikyū stops to admire the white camellias, so bright on this dark morning. He hesitates a moment, then breaks off three stems and places them inside his kimono sleeve. As he walks down the pathway that winds its way to the Kan-in teahouse, Rikyū recalls past tea ceremonies with friends, samurai, and the shōgun. Leaving his *geta* propped up against the stone step, he slides open the *nijiriguchi*, a doorway so small that the visitor must bow when entering.

> crawling in
> on hands and knees
> the Grand Tea Master

Rikyū kneels in front of the alcove where a bamboo container awaits him. Bamboo, with its agility to bend but not break, is his favorite material. The vase has faded to the color of tatami and there's a small crack at the rim. The water dipper, tea whisk, and tea scoop are also made from bamboo. All disposable and renewable. Rikyū places the container off-center so the space in the alcove will not be divided into equal halves.

The tea master gently removes the camellias from his kimono sleeve. Camellias are rarely used in flower arrangements because when they die, the entire blossom falls in one piece, like the head of a samurai being decapitated. Rikyū picks up the tallest stem, which symbolizes "heaven," and places it in the bamboo vase. At the end of the stem is a tight bud. In front of that, he places a shorter stem, "earth." This camellia is just beginning to bloom. And for the lowest level, "man," he selects a short-stemmed camellia. Its petals are open to reveal the heart of the camellia, a deep pink that radiates throughout the white petals. This is the only color in the tea room.

Rikyū has chosen a blank scroll of faded *washi* with just a few wrinkles. Once the viewer kneels directly in front of the scroll, however, he discovers that the scroll is not empty. At the upper right corner, a single bird has been rendered in quick brush strokes against the white background. It appears to be flying off the edge of the scroll, through a lavender cloud that ends at the purple silk border.

Satisfied with the flower arrangement and the scroll, Rikyū moves to the sunken hearth. He spreads a layer of ash on the bottom, then ignites three pieces of charcoal, which he lays on the bed in a triangular configuration.

wisteria twigs—
white bones of trees
ignite the charcoal

Finally, he sets the iron kettle on the hearth to boil. Taking out five tea bowls from their boxes, he lines them up on the tatami. Each bowl is a gift from a famous potter, each one unique in color and shape.

When everything has been prepared, Rikyū strikes a gong. His five guests, who have been waiting outside in an arbor, make their way along the *roji*, the "dewy path," where they empty their minds of worldly cares. Rikyū stands outside the tea house to greet them. It is a somber procession, their robes black against the snow. One by one, the disciples kneel at a water basin to rinse their hands and purify themselves. One by one, they remove their *geta* and enter the tea room through the *nijiriguchi*. Each kneels before the flowers and the scroll in the alcove. They contemplate the arrangement of camellias and the bird disappearing into the purple cloud, the cloud that accompanies the Buddha when he welcomes a dying person to his Pure Land.

Rikyū enters last and kneels at the hearth. Taking out a cloth from the folds of his kimono, he wipes the laquerware tea container and bamboo tea scoop.

the iron kettle
begins to sing
wind in the pines

Hot water is drawn from the kettle with a water ladle and poured into a bowl. Rikyū rinses the bamboo tea whisk in the bowl, empties the water, and wipes the bowl with a linen cloth. Each step is carried out with supreme concentration.

Removing the lid to the tea caddy, he places green powder into the first tea bowl. One scoop, two scoops. Slowly, he lifts the cover from the tea kettle, ladles hot water into the bowl, and whisks the tea one way and then another.

blending tea
the sound of the tea whisk
outside of time

Sen no Rikyū (1522-1591) is considered the most famous tea master in Japanese history. He introduced rustic simplicity into the traditional tea ceremony, exemplifying the qualities of harmony, respect, purity, and tranquility.

Rikyū rises, holding the tea bowl in both hands, then kneels before his first guest. They bow to one another, hands flat on tatami. Before drinking the tea, Sogan offers thanks, then turns the bowl clockwise, admiring it from all sides.

> earth and water
> fired into a tea bowl
> froth of green tea

Kneeling on the tatami, perfectly erect, Rikyū prepares four more bowls of tea. Each bowl has special significance to the guest it is presented to. Perhaps it was made in the province where he was born, or has a tubular shape like the guest's prized gourds, or an image of his favorite flower. Each disciple is honored in this way.

The final bowl is his, a heavy blue-black *raku-yaki* with an indentation on one side to break the monotony of a perfect circle. It's a deep bowl, appropriate to winter. A bowl that will hold the heat in the cold tearoom. His disciples watch as their master measures out tea, pours water, whisks the powder.

> host and guests
> breathe together
> powder becomes tea

They watch him drink his final bowl of tea, eyes closed, attentive to its fragrance and taste. When he finishes, he passes the bowl around for all to admire. A few drops of green tea remain in the bottom, like liquid jade. When the bowl has come full circle, Rikyū rinses and dries it carefully.

> slowly
> wiping the tea bowl
> no thought

To mark the end of the tea ceremony, Rikyū presents each guest with a tea bowl. One by one, each disciple receives his gift, then bows with downcast eyes. A dim light shines in through the *shōji*, highlighting the camellias and the scroll in the alcove. The room fills with silence, broken only by the call of a mourning dove.

Finally, the tea master rises, removes his outer kimono, folds it, and places it on the tatami. Sogan moves on hands and knees toward his teacher, takes the kimono, and hands him a dagger. Rikyū kneels before his guests, slowly unwrapping the dagger from its silk case.

Releasing the kimono from his shoulders and removing the undergarment, he meditates for a moment. Then, with the precision of a warrior, the Grand Tea Master thrusts the blade into his stomach. As he collapses, Sogan moves behind him and decapitates his master with a sword.

> such stillness
> after the fallen snow
> this fleeting world

The disciples prostrate themselves in grief and respect. Rising, Sogan begins to chant the *Hannya Shingyo*, the Heart Sutra, to guide Rikyū's soul to the Pure Land. The others join in. When the chanting ends, they swaddle their teacher in a white cloth and carry him outside, across the stepping stones along the snowy path.

> on the day I write
> about Sen no Rikyū's death
> first camellia blooms

Year's End

*E*very year on New Year's Eve we invite friends over to celebrate. Like the Japanese, we eat a meal of extra-long *soba* noodles for a long life and toast with *sake* drunk from small cups. Just before midnight, we bundle up and climb the hill to Yusen-ji, the oldest Nichiren sect temple. For twelve years, we have observed the Japanese year-end tradition: to eat, drink, and ring the temple bell. This will be our last New Year's in Japan.

When we arrive at the temple, families are already lined up around the bonfire. We have all come to ring the bronze bell, about eight feet high and five feet in diameter. It's struck by a horizontal swinging tree-trunk, attached to thick ropes. Japanese believe that ringing it 108 times will rid the world of the 108 sins and delusions. As I wait in line, I take out my Daruma doll, which I have brought to burn. This doll is named after a Buddhist saint who vowed to sit in meditation until he became enlightened. He was determined not to give up, even when his legs fell off. Thus, Daruma symbolizes persistence and endurance. Made of papier-maché, the dolls are round and have no legs. They are weighted so, if they are knocked over, they right themselves. Daruma dolls come in all sizes. Mine was small, only four inches tall. In keeping with Japanese tradition, I bought it on the first day of the new year, made a wish, and colored in one of his eyes. Only when you have achieved your goal do you fill in the other.

As we approach the bonfire, I lift my arm and toss Daruma into the flames. It rolls out. All the Japanese go "E-EH-e-eee?!" I pick it up and throw it back in. Out it comes again. By this time everyone is edging away from me. But, like Daruma, I too am determined. I pick it up a third time and throw it hard. This time it doesn't roll out.

> at year's end
> I burn the Daruma doll
> with only one eye

After ringing in the New Year, we walk to the Shintō shrine for the first *sake*, then home to sleep and dream the first dream of the year. A dream about Mt. Fuji brings you the most luck, a hawk second, and lastly, an eggplant.

We awaken feeling cleansed and refreshed. After breakfast, John and I open the mailbox where *nenga-jo* are waiting. The post office gathers these New Years cards until January 1st, and then delivers them all on the first day of the new year.

hanging New Year's cards
on the *shōji*
last year's dust

New Year's Day is one of the few times of the year when Japanese dress in kimono as they visit the shrine to pay their respect and to buy amulets to keep them safe throughout the year. The following days are spent socializing with family and friends.

no footprints
outside the hermit's hut
New Year's day

After the New Year's celebrations, John and I begin to make preparations to leave Kyōto. We give away or sell most of our belongings. As the house empties, it becomes more fragile. The beams seem to lean more, the tatami look shabby, and we notice for the first time that the latticed paper doors are out of kilter. All the nicks and discolorations in the walls stand out. The alcove looks forlorn with no flower arrangement or scroll. Without us and our belongings to keep it alive, the house has become the empty shell of a cicada.

leaving Japan
inside the paper lantern
a dusting of moths

THE POND IS STILL THERE, BUT SMALLER

Opening My Eyes

I first discovered Bashō's hut by chance while bicycling down narrow lanes in the eastern hills of Kyōto. Intrigued by a stone marker, I opened the gate and found myself in a temple garden. It was winter; there was nobody around. Climbing the stairs, I came upon a small dwelling where I sat on the *engawa* and wrote haiku in my notebook until the cold drove me away. Because I was unable to read the Chinese characters on the marker, I had no idea that, over three hundred years ago, both Bashō and Buson had sat in this very hut and composed haiku.

Now, years later, I return to this place of solace. The azaleas are fragrant in the balmy air. I climb up the pathway of stones made smooth by thousands of pilgrims who have come to Bashō's hut and Buson's grave. The calligraphy carved on Buson's stone is bold and elegant. As in life, the master poet is surrounded by his disciples. Their graves encircle his, as if they are preparing for a *renga* party of drinking *sake* and writing linked verses together.

> the well
> where Buson drew water
> now dry as bones

Bashō's hut is framed by new green leaves above a roof thatched with miscanthus. Once again, I sit on the termite-eaten wood of the *engawa* and look out over the city of Kyōto. Today is Children's Day and *koinobori* fly from tall poles, their colorful fish tails rippling in the wind. Very little has changed from the days when this hut was rebuilt by Buson. The four-and-a-half-mat room is empty but for a scroll and a single purple flower, which looks like an aster. Although I studied *ikebana* for twelve years, I can't identify it. Neither can the two Japanese woman who pass by, but they are happy to translate the haiku on the scroll for me:

> lying down sleeping
> I opened my eyes
> and saw the sunset

The calligraphy is brushed with a languid flow, in harmony with the mood of Buson's haiku and this simple dwelling. After the women leave, I lie down on the hard wood of the *engawa*, close my eyes, and imagine what it would be like to live here in the seventeenth century. To write, read, take naps, and awake at sunset.

> opening my eyes
> I see the beauty
> of termite wood

Dream House

*L*ast night I dreamed about my dream house. "Why are we buying a house in Japan?" I ask my husband. It has many rooms, all furnished with beautiful antiques that have been left for us. In the hallway there's a cherrywood *tansu* like one for storing kimonos, with narrow drawers. The former owner, a Japanese sage, collected soaps and the *tansu* is full of samples all labeled and numbered. I open drawer after drawer, enjoying their exotic perfume and the calligraphy on the wrappers. Then, on a more practical level, I ask if there's a washer and dryer in the house. The daughter of the sage leads me to a small room.

"Here," she says, pointing to an empty space. I smile and look out the window where I spy a small cottage.

"What's that?" I ask.

"I am not allowed to show you that place," she whispers and leaves abruptly.

From the window I have a clear view into one of the rooms, which is filled with dolls. As if on cue, two life-size dolls stand up and begin to waltz—then smaller ones, like dwarves, rise to join them. I watch the dance of the dolls for a while then turn away sadly.

"We cannot live here," I say to John, and we leave the dream house. But all day long, I find myself revisiting, one by one, all the rooms in my dream. I open the drawers of scented soap, linger at the kitchen window, and

    at dusk I watch
    a nameless bird settle
    on a tree with no leaves

Matsugasaki, Ichō da chō 10-1

Kyōto, 1997

*T*here's a bittersweet sadness about returning to a place where your memories of twelve years are centered. It's been only five years since we left, but our old traditional Japanese house in *Gaijin Mura* is totally inaccessible. The dirt lane has been cordoned off by a corrugated fence. A neighbor tells us that our landlady, Inoue-san, put up the fence after the arson. Evidently the house next to ours, occupied by our Swiss friend Ursula, was burnt to the ground. It's ridiculous to feel relieved that it wasn't ours.

Circling the fence, we find a hillock and peer over at the charred remains. I think about *higanbana*, those spiked red flowers that I gathered at the perimeter of the rice fields out back and arranged in the *tokonoma*. Japanese friends said they were unlucky—if we brought them inside, our house would burn down.

> equinox flowers
> and rice fields
> now paved over

Our house has caved in like a withered gourd. This is how it felt once we packed up all our belongings—fragile and empty. And yet, I still have this urge to go inside, to feel the familiarity of creaking doors, water-stained *fusuma*, our old cedarwood *ofuro*, and paper lanterns where moths fluttered on spring evenings. I want to sit on the tatami in the dust and rubble of an abandoned house and remember.

> cicada long since gone—
> yet, still clinging to the branch
> its abandoned husk

John locates a door in the fence and pushes it open. The lane is a tangle of kudzu weeds, overgrown trees, and yard debris tossed in by Japanese who have moved into the area. Perhaps a child could enter, crawl under the barriers, but I'm daunted. A flash of red shows through the jungle of greenery—a rusty 50cc motorbike parked in front of one of the houses. There's a red helmet attached to it. I feel a start of recognition, but it's neither my red helmet nor my motorbike.

John and I stroll around our old neighborhood and come upon one of the farmers who owns the rice fields behind our house. Matsumura-san used to wheel her cart down our dirt lane selling vegetables. She also exchanged neighborhood gossip along the way. Our nickname for her was Lady Bountiful—Lady B for short. Like a flashback, we see her loading up her cart with onions, radishes, and rape flowers to sell. John and I are overjoyed to see her after all these years and greet her warmly.

> in straw hat
> and baggy pants
> Lady Bountiful
> welcomes us, smiling
> as if we were ghosts

Orphan

*T*he houses on the lane have been abandoned and are covered with kudzu vines. We left our house in Kyōto years ago, but have come back to collect things that we neglected to take with us. At first we think we can fit them into our suitcases, but looking around at the pottery, the scrolls, and flower arrangement vases, we realize that we'll need a box. I wander around the house and come upon a section that wasn't there before—an addition, no bigger than a closet. A cushion, the size of a dog bed, has an indentation of a person curled up sleeping. I step down from the tatami into an adjoining room. It looks like a makeshift studio, with a hot plate and a few bowls. Against one wall, a wooden crate filled with kimonos. I pull them out, one by one. They are all polyester, not silk, inferior in quality and stained. There is even a rayon wedding kimono. I put them back into the crate, feeling sad. This is someone's shop or studio. On another wall, a rack of handmade cards. Some are photos of Kyōto gardens, others watercolor illustrations. A Japanese woman pokes her head in—asks who I am and why I'm here. "This used to be my house," I say.

"Yes, *gaijin* lived here. I remember. After you left, Yukio moved in. He was an orphan. Tried to make a living from selling these things." She gestures to what I have already seen. "But he couldn't, and now he is gone."

knock on the door
awakens me from my dream
rumpled kimono

Ghost of a Friend

*J*ohn and I don't give our friend much time to prepare for our surprise visit, a quick phone call from Daisen-in Temple. It's been five years since we left our old neighborhood where she still lives. Michiko was John's private Japanese-language teacher. She would often walk her dog Yuki down our lane and stop to chat. Having studied at the Sorbonne and later being married to an American for a short time, she felt relaxed with foreigners. Her traditional lineage, however, kept her anchored to Kyōto. Yuki would yip with pleasure when she saw me smoking Indonesian clove cigarettes. When I exhaled, she'd lap up the smoke.

> autumn afternoon
> old memories
> go up in smoke

Yuki died a year ago. We are prepared for our friend's sadness at losing her companion, but not for the specter that stands in the doorway. Pale-skinned, her shiny black hair faded to gray, eyes sunken into deepening shadows, Michiko greets us nervously. She twitters the formalities of *"Ohisashiburi desu"* (It's been a long time since we met) and keeps us standing in the entryway with small talk. Bundles of recycled newspapers stacked on top of one another act as a barrier to prevent anyone from entering. Though we're hot and tired, I realize that there's no possibility of being invited in for tea. Judging from her unkempt appearance, I can only imagine what her house looks like.

> the haunting tune
> of a recycling truck—
> we walk away

At the Potter's Home

*F*ive years have passed since we last visited our potter friends, the Murayamas, in Ayabe. It is unusually quiet here. Jiro the mangy dog and Goro the tomcat have died during the time we've been gone. Goro is survived by his mother Kumi, an elegant calico who spends most of her time surveying visitors from the rafters of the old farmhouse. She honors us occasionally

by allowing us to pet her, but not for long. Off she goes, hiding behind the sliding doors in Tomoko's old bedroom.

Their daughter has left for college. It is far enough from home so that neither parents nor daughter are tempted to visit on weekends. Tomoko's dolls and stuffed animals have been packed away. It's now her mother's weaving room.

> loom threaded with wool—
> her daughter's outgrown clothes
> twisted into strands

Weaving occupies Ayako in the cold months and, when it gets warmer, she gardens. And then there's Kumi. A bond has formed between the feline who lost her son and the mother whose daughter has left home. Ayako keeps track of Kumi's every movement, mews back at her, and protects her from the unwanted affection of others. It is a satisfying arrangement, one accepted by Murayama-san—husband, father, and head of the household. "Kumi is Ayako's child now," he says and goes out to the barn to throw clay.

> at the potter's home
> the cat bowl
> a work of art

The Persimmon Tree

*T*he pond is still there, but smaller. Or was it always this small and just grew larger in memory? Tall grasses grow profusely around the perimeter and wildflowers shoot up in bursts of color among them. It's a glorious spring afternoon in Ayabe. I remember coming here in every season when we lived in Kyōto, taking this same walk. Usually early morning or late afternoon, leaving Murayama's house on a path wet with dew or frost. Past the hunchbacked woman with her rickety baby carriage full of cabbage, *daikon*, or green onions, depending on the season. I never went into the graveyard because that would mean passing through a bamboo grove where poisonous *mamushi* lived.

> perfect snake name
> sinuous, secretive
> with a hiss at the end

My walk always ends at the shrine. The clearing in front of the shrine yard has been swept to welcome visitors, though the buildings are on the edge of collapse. They are cared for by old folks, who are the only ones left in the village. I shake a rope that rings the bell, then clap my palms together to call the gods. The bell's dusty rattle is in keeping with the ancient structures, moss creeping up and rotting the cedar beams of the country shrines. The carvings, simple and crude, as if done by a young child or a very old man.

It's late afternoon when I circle back. The pond is filling with shadows. I stare at the murky water and remember all the haiku I wrote here through every season. But something is different—the persimmon tree is gone. That gnarled tree, heavy with ripe persimmons, has fallen or been cut down. Years from now, when all the old people have died, the pond and tree will be forgotten—as if they never existed.

I head down the path alongside the rice fields, back to Murayama's house. The frogs have begun their croaking.

> between rows
> in the flooded paddy
> boot prints filled with mud

Sensei

*I*f we are lucky, we have a teacher in our lives who moves us along the path we need to take at the time we need to take it, someone who shows us how to live with right mind and right action. Sensei was that person for me.

Her given name was Fumiko, but all her students called her Sensei. I met her in the spring of 1981, soon after John and I arrived in Kyōto. News of my grandmother's death a continent away had just reached me, and I was grieving. With her tranquility and grace, Sensei reminded me of Nana. She even looked like her— delicate in figure, meticulously dressed, her eyes bright with the pleasure of living. And like Nana, who had a flower garden till she was ninety, Sensei had spent most of her life with flowers, teaching *ikebana*, the art of flower arrangement.

In Japanese, *sensei* means "teacher." The word carries a reverence that is no longer observed in our culture. I remember my first lesson in Sensei's room, which was packed full of students and cut flowers. Sitting beside her, I watched her select lupine, baby's breath, and ferns, cut them to a prescribed length, and arrange them in a vase. When she finished, I took out a pad and pencil and sketched the arrangement. Then, removing the flowers one by one from the needlepoint holder, I tried to replicate it. This was Sensei's method: teaching by example.

In the twelve years I studied with her, Sensei was never once critical or impatient. On winter days, she welcomed me with green tea; in the heat of summer, she offered refreshing barley tea. On the occasional afternoons when I was her only student, we would sit side by side and arrange flowers together. After praising each other's arrangement, we'd chat for a while over coffee and sweets. I didn't really care for those cakes filled with red azuki beans, but when I was with Sensei, they tasted delicious.

Returning to Kyōto

Spring 1997

I've been thinking of Sensei since we arrived in Kyōto yesterday. On the way to dinner, I feel an urgent need to see her. "I must call Sensei—now," I say to John. We stop at a coffee shop to use a pay phone. As I dial the familiar number, I think about our last lunch together five years ago, just before I left Japan—the Chinese "special ranchi" at the Fujita Hotel restaurant, overlooking a pond with swans and ducks gliding by. Then a walk along the Kamo River, where gulls flew up from the water, sunlight on their wings. We walked slowly that cold February afternoon, north to Demachi Yanagi subway station where Sensei and I parted ways. My last image of her was her small figure turning around again and again to bow and wave as she descended into the dark tunnel.

Her daughter-in-law, Shinko, answers the phone. When I ask for Sensei in Japanese, she says "Fumiko-san?" All those years I knew her only as Sensei and am startled to hear her actual name.

"It's Maggie," I say, "I've come back to visit her."

"Maggie-san, it's been a long time." Then, after a pause, she says, "Fumiko is sick."

"Oh, her allergies!" Sensei always suffered in the spring.

Shinko hesitates. "No, she has Alzheimer's." It's the same word in Japanese.

I hand the phone to John, whose Japanese is better. Leaning against the wall I'm vaguely aware of him talking on the phone, bowing words of sympathy, the laughter of couples in the background, the smell of coffee that fills the overheated room. I close my eyes and think about the past five years of sending her flower calendars, photographs, and letters from America. At first I was worried because I never heard from her, then I became angry. And all that time, Sensei was moving steadily toward darkness—a darkness, I realize now, she knew was coming.

> last time together
> I waved and said *"mata"*
> she said *"sayonara"*

Visiting Sensei
at the Alzheimer's Home

Shinko invites us to accompany her to the Alzheimer's Home to see Sensei. In Japan, it's shameful for Japanese to admit that a family member has Alzheimer's. John and I feel privileged to have Shinko's trust. We awaken early and take three trains from where we're staying to arrive at Tambabashi by ten. There is no trace of Sensei in this room where she taught flower arrangement for forty years—no needlepoint holders, no vases, no notebook where she recorded her students' monthly fees. Her son has taken over this space for his PAL English school. A lurid poster of Madonna hangs on the wall next to the 1997 Sierra Club calendar I sent her last Christmas.

During the long drive to the private hospital, Shinko keeps the conversation light, and we are too polite to ask direct questions about Sensei's condition. When we arrive, Shinko leads us through the lobby and seats us in a reception room. We watch her take the arm of a hunched-over woman and speak to her gently. How kind she is. After five years of visiting her mother-in-law, she must know everyone here. But then, Shinko leads the woman from the lobby toward the couches where we are waiting.

> hair shorn
> waddling in diapers
> my Sensei

Her face is bloated, her hair gray and clipped in prison/hospital style, which is no style at all. It is hard to look into her eyes— small slits, puffy around the lids.

> she smiles
> I smile
> tears in my eyes
> tears in hers

It's like looking into a mirror. Having no emotions of her own, Sensei mimics mine. Shinko explains that she is the only one that Sensei recognizes. How terrible for the son and daughter and grand-daughters.

"Where are her glasses?" I ask, as Sensei squints at me.

> losing her glasses
> picking up the glasses
> of other patients—
> still can't recognize
> anyone

> > what does she see
> > when she stares at this stranger
> > weeping in front of her?

> > > "Over there, over there"
> > > she says looking toward
> > > the direction I turn
> > > to wipe away my tears

> > > > turning away
> > > > I listen to her voice
> > > > and know it is her

Shinko goes out and brings back cans of Coca Cola from a vending machine for us and helps her mother-in-law drink a cup of green tea. I take out the photo album I brought with me to show Sensei our lives in Oregon. Slowly, Shinko, John, and I leaf through the album hoping to make some connection.

> showing her photographs
> she watches us
> looking at ourselves

> no sense of time
> no sense of seasons
> now is forever

Putting away the photo album, I reach into my bag and take out the package of soap I brought for her.

> presenting her soap
> wrapped in peony paper—
> her birthday flower

Her hands are still the same. Small fingers, delicate, yet strong enough to cut through a thick branch for a flower arrangement. I always loved those hands. She holds the cake of soap like a flower, like the bouquet of peonies I gave her with a haiku on her seventieth birthday:

> spreading its sweetness
> the thousand-petaled flower
> *shakuyaku*

> packaged like cakes
> this rose-scented soap
> so good to eat

after the mothballs
they checked her
into the hospital

Shinko gently takes the soap away from Sensei. I speak to her in simple English, as in the old days, hoping to join the pieces together like a jigsaw puzzle, to unlock her memories. But I soon realize that even her Japanese makes no sense.

"Maggie, Maggie" I repeat
she stares at me blankly, says
"Over there, over there!"

At our good-bye lunch at the Fujita Hotel, Sensei gave me an expensive leather wallet. As I thanked her effusively, she reached into her handbag and took out her own wallet. It was exactly like mine. "My daughter gave this to me for my birthday. I'm giving you the same wallet so every time you open it, you will think of me. And when I open mine, I will remember you."

I show her the wallet
she presented me
at our last farewell

she stares at me hard
—remembering how
we never needed words

The old folks are shuffling, wheel chairing, being helped into the dining room for lunch. They all look much worse than Sensei, completely spiritless. Yet I cannot be heartened by her sturdiness. I know it is only a matter of time until she becomes like them, just as I know that this will be the last time I see her.

for the final photo
she smiles, I weep
no memory, memory

   not knowing
   what she has lost
   —what is happy?

      holding her hand
      into the dining room then
       letting her go

         she cranes her neck
         to watch me leave
         I wave and wave
           and wave

Tōfuku-ji Zen Garden

ohn and I thank Shinko for bringing us to visit Sensei, then board a train bound for Tōfuku Temple. Disembarking amidst hoards of black-uniformed high school students, we duck under an indigo curtain into a noodle shop. *"Irashai!"* the owner welcomes us. At 2:00, the shop has few customers, only some locals reading the newspaper or watching the huge television which looms over the room. It is cool and dark here after walking in the afternoon heat. We order *zarusoba*, which arrives on a bamboo mat placed on a lacquerware box. On television, a samurai drama is in full swing—nobles and warlords dash from one tatami room in the castle to another, scheming intricate plots. Every actor has mastered "the look," a wordless understanding transmitted through eye contact. Women with waist-length hair weep over the death of a husband, brother, lover—we foreigners cannot tell which in this complexity of feudal relationships. And we have tuned in too late to have any hope of following the plot. Yet, it is somehow soothing to be wrapped in this cocoon of coolness watching men and women of another era suffer and not understand why.

Refreshed, we make our way uphill to the fifteenth-century temple complex of Tōfuku-ji. The *hōjo*, head priest's quarters, has a modern-style Zen garden which we've never seen. Hoards of noisy students have moved on and we have the place to ourselves. John walks around taking photographs while I sit on the veranda and mourn Sensei. As I contemplate the emptiness of these stones, I try to imagine what it would be like to lose all memory.

non-attachment
nothing
to attach to

dry stone garden
holding memories
between the cracks

watching old women
enjoy the azaleas
why them, not her?

I bend down to smell
their faint fragrance
for her

bamboo sways in the wind
wishing I could erase
this memory

water drips
into an empty basin
her life passes

Camellias

For the Japanese, the first dream of the new year *(hatsuyume)* is an auspicious one. This year I dreamed that I had received a package from Japan. Curious, I opened the box immediately. Inside, carefully wrapped in pastel-colored tissue paper, were Sensei's *ikebana* scissors. I knew they were hers because she always tied a gold or silver string around one of the handles to distinguish them from those of her students. At first I was delighted and honored to receive Sensei's scissors, but then I realized that this was her daughter-in-law's way of telling me that Sensei had died.

All morning I held that dream close, trying to recall every detail, savoring the intimacy and spiritual connection with Sensei. When the rain eased, I took the sheath off my own *ikebana* scissors and headed outside. It was New Year's Day and I wanted to make a flower arrangement for Sensei. As I clipped camellias, I thought about all those afternoons together arranging flowers, talking, and drinking tea. And how she had always put aside the best flowers for me. Camellias would probably not be appropriate for a New Year's arrangement, as some Japanese believe they bring bad luck if brought into the house. But I was not in Japan and, more importantly, Sensei taught me to use whatever materials were at hand. The camellias—pink, red, and white—with their shiny green leaves looked festive against the gray Portland landscape. I held the bouquet in my left hand, scissors poised in my right. Thinking about this morning's dream, I looked closely at the shears, their blades chipped and rusty from years of use. And there, frayed but still attached to one of the handles, was a silver string.

> clipping camellias
> with Sensei's old scissors
> a new year begins

Glossary

ajisai	hydrangeas
bashō	banana tree, the nom de plume of haiku poet Matsuo Bashō
biwa	four-stringed Japanese lute
bulbul	common scruffy gray and brown bird, similar to a jay
chabana	simple seasonal flowers for tea ceremony
daikon	large white radish
daimyō	lords and rulers of feudal clans
engawa	a floor extension at one side of a Japanese-style house or temple, usually facing a garden
fusuma	a framed and papered sliding door used to partition off a room
futon	traditional Japanese bedding consisting of a flat mattress stuffed with cotton and laid out on the floor
gaijin	literally "outside people;" used to describe Caucasians
genkon	entryway of a Japanese house or temple
geta	traditional Japanese sandals
gobo	burdock root
haiga	haiku and painting paired, as seen on a scroll
haori	silk jacket worn over a kimono
hara-kiri	suicide by disembowelment
hibachi	large ceramic urn containing charcoal; often placed in temples for guests to warm their hands over as they view the garden

higanbana	flower of the autumn equinox
hina dolls	a set of ornamental dolls displayed on March 3 for Girls' Day
hondo	the main hall for worship in a Japanese temple
hotaru	firefly
ikebana	Japanese art of flower arrangement
irashai	welcome greeting when you enter a restaurant or shop
Jataka	Buddhist teaching tales or fables
-ji	temple, as in Ryōan-ji
jinja	shrine
kampai	Japanese equivalent of "cheers" said before a toast
kanji	Chinese system of writing adopted by the Japanese
karesansui	dry landscape garden
kigo	a seasonal word used in haiku
kirei	beautiful
koinobori	carp streamers flown on poles to celebrate Children's Day on May 5
kokeshi	wooden dolls with no arms or legs, believed to be good luck charms
konbanwa	good evening
kotatsu	low wooden table covered by a heavy blanket with a heater below
koto	Japanese zither with fourteen strings
kura	traditional Japanese storehouses for precious items or rice
mala	prayer beads for Buddhist meditation practice

mamushi	a small venomous pit viper
marga	"the path to enlightenment" in Sanskrit
mata	see you again soon
miso	soybean paste used for making soup or sauces
mompei	indigo-dyed cotton or hemp pants worn by women working in the fields
nabe	one-pot dishes cooked at the table during the cold season
nakodo	go-between for an arranged marriage
Namu Amida Butsu	"Hail to Amida Buddha" chanted by Japanese Pure Land Buddhists
nengajo	postcard-size New Year's cards featuring the Chinese zodiac animal for the year
nijiriguchi	literally "crawl-in space" where the guests enter for a tea ceremony
obi	sash worn with a kimono
Ono no Komachi	Heian era waka poet (825-900) renowned for her beauty
parinirvana	Mahayana Buddhist festival that marks the death of the Buddha.
renga	linked verse written between two or more haiku poets
roji	literally "dewy path;" the garden area through which the guests walk to reach the tea house
sabi	rustic simplicity
sake	fermented rice wine
sasa	sound of wind in bamboo
satori	sudden enlightenment in Zen Buddhism
sayonara	good-bye

sensei	teacher
sento	public bath
shakuyaku	peony
shōji	sliding wooden door comprised of an open lattice covered with a single layer of translucent paper
Shōwa era	the reign of the Emperor Hirohito, from 1926 to 1989
soba	buckwheat noodles
tabi	formal, pure white socks, divided like a mitten
tansu	Japanese chest
tanuki	Japanese raccoon dog
tatami	woven matted floors found in traditional Japanese homes and in temples
tokonoma	an alcove in the main room where a scroll and flower arrangement are displayed
tombi	long black woolen coat worn by elderly Japanese men
torii	entry gate to a Shinto shrine
tsuyu	rainy season, lasting approximately from June 5– July 20
waka	a classical-era poem written in five lines with a 5-7-5-7-7 syllable count, now known as tanka.
washi	Japanese paper made from the wood pulp of the mulberry bush
zarusoba	a chilled noodle dish made from buckwheat flour and served with a soy and lime dipping sauce

Acknowledgments

I am greatly indebted to Lynn Connor and John Hall for their careful reading of the manuscript and for offering invaluable comments. Thanks also to Judy Montgomery for suggestions on the Introduction and to Scott Russell Sanders and Patricia Hampl who encouraged me to pursue this project during my residency at the Vermont Studio Center.

Much appreciation to Playa at Summer Lake, The Helene Wurlitzer Foundation, the Vermont Studio Center, and Hypatia-in-the-Woods for supporting my work by offering me residencies and fellowships.

My sincere thanks to Oregon Literary Arts, which awarded me a Fellowship in Creative Nonfiction for an earlier version of *Firefly Lanterns*.

A deep bow to John Einarsen for his sublime photographs, which add a visual aesthetic to the book.

And, lastly, thank you Christine Cote, founder and publisher of Shanti Arts. It has been a pleasure working with you.

Grateful acknowledgement to the editors of the following journals and anthologies where these *haibun* first appeared:

Bottle Rockets: "At the Potter's Home," "Hexed," "Opening My Eyes," and "The Persimmon Tree"

Contemporary Haibun Online (CHO): "The Great Hermit Temple"

Frogpond: "Faint Profiles," "The Monk of Amida-ji," and "The Weight of Stones"

Grandmother's Pearls (An Anthology of Dream Poems), Jade Mountain Press, 2021: "Dream of Ablutions"

Grinding my ink, Katsura Press, 1993: "Plum Rain" (haiku)

Hermitage Journal (Romania): "Meditation on *Sarasōju*" and "Rikyū's Last Tea"

Journeys 2015: An Anthology of International Haibun, edited by Angelee Deodhar (Chandigarh, India): "Bewitched by *Tanuki*," "Opening my Eyes," and "The Weight of Stones"

Kansai Time Out (Japan): *"Namu Amida Butsu"*

Kyōto Journal (Japan): "A Gathering of Souls," "Meditation on *Sarasōju*," and "Sensei"

Modern Haiku: "Mud Dreams," *"Nezumi* Jet Coaster," "Koha the Sacred Horse," and *"Yū-mo-a"*

Shadow Lines, Katsura Press, 1999: "Dream House"

Simply Haiku: "Orphan"

Talus and Scree: "At the *Sentō*"

This Moment, Katsura Press, 1995: Haiku from "Rikyū's Last Tea"

The Unswept Path: An Anthology of American Haiku Poets, White Pine Press, 2005: "At Year's End," "Bewitched by *Tanuki*," and "Firefly Lanterns"

VoiceCatcher: A Journal of Women's Voices & Visions: "Lovers, Molesters, and Maidens"

Awards

"A Gathering of Souls" won First Prize in the Annual *Kansai Time Out* Writing Contest, 1985

"Well of Beauty" was awarded the Grand Prix in the 2014 Genjuan International Haibun Contest (Kyōto, Japan)

"The Monk of Amida-ji" received an Honorable Mention in the 2013 Genjuan International Haibun Contest (Kyōto, Japan)

Images

All images are used with permission of the photographer.

About the Author

 Margaret Chula grew up on her grandparent's tobacco farm on the banks of the Connecticut River, where she explored eighty acres of woods and meadows. In her thirties, she traveled around the world with her husband and then settled in Kyōto for twelve years, where she taught English and creative writing at universities. Maggie has published twelve collections of poetry, including *Grinding my ink*, which received the Haiku Society of America Book Award, and *One Leaf Detaches*, a 2019 Touchstone Distinguished Book Award winner. She has been a featured speaker and workshop leader at writers' conferences throughout the United States, as well as in Poland, Canada, Ireland, Peru, and Japan. In 2010, she was appointed Poet Laureate for Friends of Chamber Music in Portland, Oregon. She also served for five years as President of the Tanka Society of America and currently sits on the Advisory Board of the Center for Japanese Studies at Portland State University. Grants from Oregon Literary Arts and the Regional Arts and Culture Council have supported collaborations with artists, musicians, photographers, and dancers. She lives in Portland, Oregon, where she hikes, gardens, swims, and creates flower arrangements for every room of the house.

SHANTI ARTS

NATURE · ART · SPIRIT

Please visit us online
to browse our entire book catalog,
including poetry collections and fiction,
books on travel, nature, healing, art,
photography, and more.

Also take a look at our highly
regarded art and literary journal,
Still Point Arts Quarterly, which
may be downloaded for free.

www.shantiarts.com

CPSIA information can be obtained
at www.ICGtesting.com
Printed in the USA
BVHW020729160921
616188BV00016B/45